LOUDER THAN WORDS

LOUDER
THAN WORDS

JENNY McCARTHY

BANTAM PRESS

LONDON · TORONTO · SYDNEY · AUCKLAND · JOHANNESBURG

TRANSWORLD PUBLISHERS
61–63 Uxbridge Road, London W5 5SA
A Random House Group Company
www.rbooks.co.uk

First published in Great Britain in 2008 by Bantam Press
an imprint of Transworld Publishers

This book is a work of non-fiction based on the life, experiences and recollections of Jenny McCarthy.

The health-related materials in this book are for informational or educational purposes only. You should not rely on this information as a substitute for the advice of your health-care professionals. Please consult them regarding the applicability of any opinions or recommendations in this book with respect to any symptoms or medical conditions that you or your family may experience.

While the author has made every effort to provide accurate telephone numbers and internet addresses at the time of publication, neither the publisher nor the author assumes any responsibility for errors, or for changes that occur after publication. Further, the publisher does not have any control over and does not assume any responsibility for author or third-party websites or their content.

A CIP catalogue record for this book
is available from the British Library.

ISBN 9780593061701

Addresses for Random House Group Ltd companies outside the UK
can be found at: www.randomhouse.co.uk
The Random House Group Ltd Reg. No. 954009

The Random House Group Limited supports The Forest Stewardship
Council (FSC), the leading international forest-certification organization. All our
titles that are printed on Greenpeace-approved FSC-certified paper carry the FSC logo.
Our paper procurement policy can be found at www.rbooks.co.uk/environment

Printed in the UK by CPI Mackays, Chatham, ME5 8TD

2 4 6 8 10 9 7 5 3 1

～

Evan:

When I asked you what you wanted to
be when you grew up, you said, "A flower."

I can't think of anything better.

You are the most beautiful flower I have
ever seen, and I'm the luckiest mom in the
world to be able to watch you bloom into the
most radiant flower God has ever made.

I love you.

Mommy

⌒

Special thanks to:

H. P. for teaching me about the window. I will never forget
our conversation that night, and I hope you know how many
families you've helped because of it.

Also

Trena Keating, Brian Tart, and Jennifer Rudolph Walsh,
I couldn't have asked God for a better publishing team.

And

all the beautiful therapists and people who have helped
open that window and help keep it open.
We couldn't have done it without you!
Speech Sarah, Jenny, Tonya, Paul, Maritza, Anthony,
Chris, John L., Kim, Sam, Johno, New Sarah, Jenna, Alex, Myra,
Crystal, Doug, Eric, Kristen, Lisa M., Lisa A., Dr. Shields,
Dr. Sarah Spence, Dr. Kartzinel, Dr. Gordon, Dr. Kaplan,
and the Mormons.

Foreword

∾

WHEN YOUR CHILD is diagnosed with cancer, neighbors stop by your home bringing precooked meals, hugs, and support. When your child is diagnosed with autism, families who see you in the supermarket will slip away down another aisle.

WHAT IS AUTISM?

Autism is a disorder that now affects one in a hundred and fifty children. When I was in medical school, this disorder affected one in ten thousand children. These children have problems with language development and usage. They have rituals and repetitive behaviors. They have problems understanding how to interact socially. The spectrum of severity is broad. Some are severely afflicted and need institutional care, while others are only "brushed" with the disorder and grow up, work, marry, and have children of their own. Those with autism have higher rates of epilepsy and increased rates of mental retardation.

WHAT IS THE TREATMENT?

Treatment for this now all-too-common disorder is rather limited. Behavioral therapies, along with speech and occupational therapy, are the cornerstone of care. Traditional Western medications have minimal value. Aggressive behavior can be controlled partially with medication.

Controversy exists regarding the use of diet restriction for treatment and the role of vaccines and mercury in causation. Over time, many alternative approaches to autism have come and gone, refuted by the medical establishment. But remember, the medical establishment used to believe that autism was caused by uncaring parents or "refrigerator moms." Many families with autistic children believe that some of these less traditional interventions have made significant positive changes in their children.

Treatments that have been shown to be effective, such as speech and behavioral therapy, are frequently not available because of waiting lists, insurance restrictions, or a lack of appropriately trained professionals. Diagnosis is often delayed or missed because of lack of screening, minimizing developmental delays, or lack of knowledge among health care providers.

Everyone agrees that early intervention is critical.

WHAT IS NORMAL?

At about five weeks of age, babies smile for the first time. I think that this is so because our ancestors threw away the babies who hadn't smiled by this time. Anyone who has parented knows how physically hard it is to care for a newborn. Finally, after nights of feedings, burpings, and diapers, our kids look at us and crack a smile (likely because they have gas), and all of sudden you feel that it is all worth it. Why does a smile back at the exhausted parent mean so much? It is because we are social beings, and this new human is recognizing us. Over the first year of life, facial expressions and other nonverbal cues (pointing a finger at something) join the baby with Mom and Dad. Then language, another extremely important milestone, develops. Over the next few years, play becomes so important. First play is in parallel: This means that two children sit next to each other, each playing independently. Next, play becomes interactive and imaginative: Children use make-believe and one another in their play. Kids in grade school form "clubs" and "cliques." They perform make-believe marriages. It seems like everything is going so well—and then they become teens.

HOW ARE CHILDREN WITH AUTISM DIFFERENT?

Children with autism don't make eye contact in the same way normally developing children do. They don't smile when they are supposed to. They don't come to you when they get hurt. They may even self-inflict pain. Their language is not only delayed, it can be deviant. They may refer to themselves in the third person or misuse pronouns. They can be hypersensitive to sounds or touch. Their play is not functional. Instead of playing with the toy truck, they spin a wheel endlessly. Interactive and make-believe play is very slow to develop, if it does at all. These kids spin, flap, and toe-walk. Other kids ignore or tease the autistic child in grade school. The phone doesn't ring for playdates. The autistic child really gets lost in the subtle social complexities of middle school and high school.

WHAT CAUSES AUTISM, AND WHY IS IT INCREASING?

Even the best minds in the field are unable to agree on answers. Genetics are probably involved: We see families in which more than one sibling is affected. The environment also probably plays a role. But what exactly that role is, no one knows for sure, and how the genetics and environment interact is the big question. The increasing rate is also an enigma, with many differing opinions.

WHO IS JENNY?

If we called mothers "refrigerator moms" in the past, then Jenny McCarthy is the polar opposite. She is the warm, glowing fireplace burning on the most beautiful winter day. In this book, she takes us on a journey of a mom dealing with her son's autism diagnosis and treatment. On this journey, we discover many things. We learn what it is like to be a parent and have your dreams shattered. We learn how the medical profession needs to remember bedside manner. We learn about healing, hope, and faith. We learn about a disease and about how others dealing with similar circumstances can aid one another. We learn about alternative approaches that seem promising. We learn that being famous doesn't mean things come easy.

Desperation, conflict, passion, humor, sadness, anger, compassion, elation, and hope are just some of the emotions that Jenny shares. Jenny's connection to her son is so strong that she practically has a seizure when he does, even when she is miles away. Jenny is affectionate, kind, parental, protective, and proactive in a crisis. Jenny's maternal connection and instincts define motherhood. It is truly not just *louder than words,* it is *stronger than words*.

By baring her soul and sharing her story, Jenny McCarthy will certainly help those who can relate because a loved one has autism, Asperger's, or some other neurodevelopmental disorder. But Jenny may be doing something even grander. My hope is that this journey will affect those without a direct connection to autism, too. My vision is that through this story, these nonafflicted families won't dodge those with an autistic child in the supermarket or at the mall, but rather embrace these children and families with compassion, support, and prayer.

David Feinberg, MD, MBA
Medical Director, Resnick Neuropsychiatric Hospital at UCLA

Introduction

∽

"YOU BROKE HIM, now you fix him!" was the mandate given to me by my wife as we watched our fourth boy slip into the world of autism after receiving his first mumps, measles, and rubella (MMR) vaccine. Seeing no other viable option in my medical textbooks, I, like so many other parents, embarked on the journey of interventions that would allow our son to leave his autistic world and rejoin ours. Autism in our home, as in every home, was a 24/7 experience: the screaming, the sleepless nights, the bloated belly, the constipation, the diarrhea, the ear infections (and the accompanying antibiotics), the obsessions/perseverations/rigidity, and of course, the heartbreaking loss of eye contact, loss of language, and loss of play skills. I was and am amazed at the lethargic response of the medical community to the escalating crisis/epidemic called autism. I couldn't wait. The bottom line in my home was the recovery of my child.

My "formal" training in pediatrics took place in the

1980s. I distinctly remember one of my mentors pointing out an autistic child who had come to our clinic. "Isn't he cool?" he commented. "You'll probably never see another; they're extremely rare." Something has radically changed since that time. These children can now be seen everywhere. But since autism affects about five males for every female, this statistic can be rewritten to remove the influence of female children: one boy in seventy boys. That is staggering! So why doesn't the general pediatrician get involved?

Well, as long as autism is considered a mental disorder or a genetic disorder, then the list of referral specialists is quite predictable: neurologist, geneticist, behavioral pediatrician, psychiatrist, and a therapist for the mom, since most of the issues are her "fault," anyway. But you know what? Despite all the evaluations and platitudes, the child somehow improves only minimally, if at all.

Autism, as I see it, steals the soul from a child; then, if allowed, relentlessly sucks life's marrow out of the family members, one by one. It relegates every other "normal" thing to utter insignificance. Inevitably, the question bubbles up through the muck: "What do I do with my anger, my pain, my frustration, my grief?" Time to roll up my general-pediatric sleeves and put all my training to work.

If I looked at each system that is not working, and treated it, then maybe I could fix one thing at a time. Starting with my own son, I had to fix the nutritional aberrations (he was consuming only chocolate chip cookies, french fries, Froot Loops, and half a gallon of milk per day). Fixing his diet required the removal of gluten-containing foods and all forms of dairy. What we then experienced was staggering. We saw sleepless nights morph into complete and glorious SLEEP! By adding cod liver oil to his diet, we witnessed the return of eye contact and language! Hey, maybe this autism is *treatable*. Finding out what is broken and fixing it may truly be the key to recovery.

It's amazing to watch children improve when the causes of their pain (screaming!), diarrhea, constipation, and frequent illnesses are removed. It is exciting to hear from parents that stimming behavior is gone, that seizures are few and infrequent. It's exciting for me to see hope return to the parents. Marriages restored. Families restored. The autistic child can come back to our world!

Jenny has done an incredible job retelling the story of Evan, who has also made the perilous journey through autism. One cannot underestimate the impact of environmental exposures, whether natural or man-made (no matter how good the intent may be) on the developing brain and body of a child from conception on. More important, one must never, never give up on the repair process. Autism is treatable!

Autism is not a dead-end diagnosis. It is the beginning of a journey into faith, hope, love, and recovery.

Jerry J. Kartzinel, MD, FAAP
Board-certified Pediatrician
Pediatric Partners of Ponte Vedra
www.pppvonline.com

LOUDER THAN WORDS

Chapter 1

∾

THE MOMENT I OPENED my eyes that morning, I had an uncomfortable feeling. It was as if my soul had the flu. I hurt inside, but I knew I wasn't getting sick, so I got out of bed and shook it off as I shuffled into the kitchen for some coffee. My mom was in town and already enjoying her morning brew. I always wished she could live in Los Angeles with me, but she was still a full-time custodian back in Chicago, and retirement for her still seemed far away. I enjoyed seeing her sweet smile and treasured every minute I got to spend with her. I was glad my son, Evan, was sleeping a little late this morning so I had time to catch up with her on all the usual gossip that was going on in my old neighborhood. As I took a moment to enjoy my first sip of coffee, I heard a voice in my head. It said, "Evan never sleeps in this late."

I stopped midsip and looked at the clock. The voice was right. Evan always woke up at seven A.M. almost to the second, and it was seven forty-five. I put down my coffee and told my mom I was going to check on him. As I walked down the hall, that sick feeling in my soul started up again. As I got closer to his room, my heart started beating fast. I couldn't understand what was going on. I started running toward his room and threw open his door. The sound I heard will be imprinted on my soul forever: my son struggling to breathe. I ran to the crib and saw my son fighting to take in air. I grabbed him in my arms and started screaming at the top of my lungs, "Something is wrong with Evan. Oh my God, help me!"

I ran his limp body into the living room while his father, John, leaped to call 911. I laid Evan down in the living room and ripped off all his clothes. My mother was screaming while Evan convulsed and wheezed. I looked into his eyes, which were wide open, and saw that one pupil was dilated and the other was small. I kept shouting, "What's wrong with him? What's *wrong with him?*"

I didn't know what to do. His skin looked white, and his lips were no longer rosy pink. I put my lips next to his ear and said, "Stay with me, baby, stay with me. Mama's here." Thoughts of having a brain-damaged child flew through my head. I feared I would never again see him do all his cute little things. I wanted Evan back. I wanted this to *stop*.

Finally, after the longest fourteen minutes in my life, I saw the paramedics casually walking up my driveway. I ran outside and screamed, "Don't fucking walk. Get over here, run!"

They picked up the pace but began to talk about my son

casually, as if they were at the office watercooler. I heard one of them say "seizure," and that didn't make sense. Don't seizures last only a minute or so? I didn't know how long Evan had been seizing when I found him, but he had been seizing the entire fifteen minutes it took the paramedics to get here. That would be one hell of a seizure. There was no history of seizures in our family. I was confused.

They had a hard time getting an IV in him because his body was convulsing. I kept yelling at the paramedics to make it stop. I saw the look on John's face and saw how scared he was, too. After a few failed attempts, they got the needle in Evan's vein and began to inject him with some fluid. Moments later, his body stopped convulsing, and his breathing went back to normal. He was now unconscious. I stood there, numb. One of the paramedics looked at me and said, "Who's coming with us in the ambulance? We can only fit one."

I quickly replied, "Me."

There was no time for arguing with John as to who got to sit in the ambulance. I was so grateful he didn't put up a fight. He quickly replied, "I'll follow behind."

The paramedic looked down at my clothing and said, "Okay, then, why don't you go change and meet us out at the ambulance."

I looked down and saw I was still wearing my flannel Bugs Bunny pajamas. I replied, "I'm fine in this. Let's go."

A paramedic lightly took my arm and walked me into the other room. "It's gonna take a few minutes to figure out which hospital we're taking him to. Now go change." With that, I ran into my closet. I couldn't see straight and grabbed anything that didn't have cartoons on it. I ran back outside as they were putting Evan in the back of the ambulance. When I got in the passenger seat up front, I saw everyone on my block standing on their stoop with a hand over their mouth, shaking their head. There is nothing worse than seeing a young child being put in the back of an ambulance.

When we got on the freeway, it was bumper-to-bumper traffic. We were stuck in the worst part of morning rush hour. I kept yelling at the driver to do something, and he said there was nothing he could do. There were no shoulders on the freeway. At last I made him get off and take side streets, but they were no better. It was shocking to see how many people completely ignore an ambulance coming through; they don't get out of the way. If I'd had a gun, I would have murdered many selfish people on the road that day. After thirty-five minutes, we arrived at the hospital. They wheeled in Evan, and the barrage of questions began.

"How old is he?"

"He's two and a half."

"Did your son have a temperature?"

"No, not that I'm aware of," I replied.

"Do seizures run in the family?"

"No, not at all," I said.

"Was he injured in any way?"

"No, I found him in his crib like this," I said.

They began a number of tests, taking blood and checking his pupils. I sat on his bed and rubbed my hand softly over his forehead. I sang the lullaby I'd sung to him as a baby and prayed to God my boy would wake up and say, "Mama."

John and my mother arrived. The looks on their faces were so sad. I couldn't even imagine what I might have looked like to them. We really didn't do much talking. We all stayed focused on the little angel lying in the bed in front of us.

HOURS HAD PASSED, and still nothing from Evan. The doctor came in and said they were going to do a CAT scan to rule out a brain tumor. I shook at the possibility of a diagnosis like that. I watched as Evan was wheeled into the CAT scan room, and I waited for the results. They came back negative. Thank God. Thank you, God. There was no tumor!

Another three hours had passed, and still nothing from my boy. I was starting to freak out because I couldn't understand why, six hours after having a seizure, he still hadn't opened his eyes. Another doctor came in the room and told me they wanted to test him for meningitis, since sometimes seizures and meningitis go hand in hand. After I agreed, they told me that the test would require a needle going into his spine to take out fluid. I became queasy just thinking about Evan going through anything else, but I knew it had to be done.

They usually sedate kids when they do this procedure, and since Evan was still not awake, they wanted to do it soon. But I learned that "soon" on hospital terms can mean "on the next shift change." After another hour of waiting, I noticed Evan's eyes begin to flutter. Tears filled my own eyes as I whispered, "Hey, little bird, it's Mama."

His eyes looked stoned and vacant. Even though I was happy he was awake, my heart sank at the loss of his soul in his eyes. I wanted Evan back. I didn't want to wait. I tried again. "Hey, little bird, it's mama bird."

His eyes rolled back and to the left and just stayed there. He still looked very pasty, and I shouted out to the nurses. They came over and started to shake him with a little force to bring him out of the lost world he was in.

"Hello, Evan, can you see your mama? Can you look at your mama?" They shouted this umpteen times with no luck. Moments later, his eyes shut, and he was out again. I didn't know what to make of it. Was that all I had left of my son? Even the doctors looked worried. It had been eight hours since the seizure, and he was still not alert. I prayed to God and said He could take me sooner if He would just make my boy better. I crawled into bed next to Evan and cried so hard. Once again, his eyes began to flutter. This time, though, he was making direct eye contact. He looked right into my eyes. I smiled the biggest smile I could and got right up to his face and said, "Hi, Evan. It's Mama!"

He stared at me with no response. It seemed like he did not recognize who I was. He just watched me and my movements. The doctors all came back over and were sticking lights in his eyes and poking and pinching parts of his body to see if that stimulated a response. It did. He started crying and then looked at me and said the most beautiful word I had ever heard: "Mama." I burst into tears and hugged him. He still was not himself and couldn't really respond to anything else, but at that moment I didn't care. He saw me and said, "Mama."

They did a few more stimulating tests and then told me they were ready to do the meningitis test.

"What the hell are you talking about?" I asked. "He just woke up after eight hours, and you want to poke him in the back and suck out some spinal fluid? Besides, he's awake now, and there is no way I'm letting you sedate him after he was out for so long."

They agreed that they wouldn't sedate him. They had a different plan. They wanted to do the procedure on him while he was awake and alert. I started to freak out. I didn't know what to do. It was so difficult to be in this kind of a situation, when you have to make a horrific decision with no good options. The doctors told John and me that this was the only way to be sure about meningitis, and it had to be done. We both painfully agreed. I asked John, if he would be the one to be with Evan for the procedure. One of the parents had to hold him down and not let him move at all. I knew I didn't have the heart to see my baby get a needle jabbed into his spine; I just couldn't do it. So I kissed Evan and handed him over to John and left the room. I ran down the hallway and sat down in a corner and buried my head in my lap and cried. I wanted this to be over. I wanted to wake up and start the day all over again. Ten minutes later, my mom picked me up off the floor and said, "It's all over, baby. Everything went fine."

The doctors returned with the test results and said that he did not have meningitis, but just in case, they were going to give him the same HUGE antibiotic injection they would have given someone with meningitis. That didn't make sense to me at all, but I agreed because there's nothing wrong with getting an antibiotic when you don't really need one, right? Wrong!

THEY ADMITTED US overnight, and the next morning a young Doogie Howser neurologist came in the room to examine Evan before releasing him from the hospital. The neurologist said he'd had a febrile seizure and to rotate between Tylenol and Motrin every three hours. I stopped the neurologist middiagnosis and said, "I'm sorry, I thought febrile seizures happen when a child has a fever. My son had no fever and wasn't sick." (I knew this by going online when Evan was a baby and researching fevers and how to care for them. I had come across information on febrile seizures.)

He replied, "Well, you never know—he could have been getting sick and it went away." Okay, can you believe that explanation? "He could have been sick and it went away"? I stood there in shock and silence because I couldn't think of a polite way to say, "You're a fucking idiot."

I got Evan dressed while we waited for John to pick us up. I asked John to buy Evan a big-boy bed and to destroy his crib. I never wanted to see that crib again for the rest of my life. When it was time to leave, I put Evan on his feet, and he immediately fell over. He had no sense of balance whatsoever and was even acting kooky. He didn't talk much, and his behavior was odd. It really worried me that he couldn't walk in a straight line. I carried him to the car and was so relieved to be leaving the hospital and the whole horrible experience. I was bringing my boy home, and I prayed that he would be back to his old self again soon.

Walking into our house was bittersweet. I was happy to be there but also sickened by the memory of the events that had taken place under this roof the day before. I wish I could say that this was the end and the seizure happened to be a fluke. But in fact, this was only the beginning.

Chapter 2

∽

The Worst of the Worst

DURING THE NEXT WEEK, I found myself, over and over again, reliving the moment of finding my son in the crib, convulsing and fighting to breathe. I even reenacted walking down that hallway because I thought it might help me let it go. It didn't help, but they say time heals everything, so I was counting on that.

I noticed that Evan was still a little different. It took him a full week to find his balance again, and even then he walked like he had vertigo. I decided to start doing some research—and by research, I mean Google. By the end of the book, you will see that I should have a doctorate in Google research, what with all the time I spent online trying desperately to understand what was happening to my baby.

First, I learned more about febrile seizures, just to be prepared. The more I read, the more the info reaffirmed for me how wrong that diagnosis was. Nonetheless, I learned on Google that once a child has a febrile seizure, the likelihood of his having another one is high. I was scared. Since we had come home from the hospital, I had spent every night in my son's bed, with one hand on his chest, afraid to fall asleep. How the hell was I ever supposed to be able to sleep a sound night for the rest of my life? The last seizure had been so quiet, I couldn't hear it on the baby monitor when I was awake and listening for him.

After three weeks had gone by, I slowly started to feel better. Easter was coming up, and we had planned a three-hour car ride down to Palm Springs to visit John's mom and stepfather and hunt for Easter eggs. I decided to leave my sorrows behind and bring only happiness on this trip. Little did I know, the worst moment in my life was about to unfold. Easter will forever be haunted for me by the events that you are about to read.

We packed up the car and decided to leave at Evan's bedtime, thinking he would fall asleep on the drive. He was still acting a bit kooky—and borderline annoying. He kept screaming and tantruming most of the day, so John and I thought it was a good plan to have him sleep through the drive so we could have some downtime. Once we were on the freeway, I looked up and saw a beautiful harvest moon. It was so big, it made me laugh, and Evan was mesmerized by how it followed us the whole drive. I was so happy to get out of L.A. and looked forward to watching Evan have some fun with the Easter Bunny. John's mom always threw the best holiday parties, so I knew this one was gonna be good. Evan hadn't gotten to know these grandparents well yet because they lived in a different city, so I thought it would be a great bonding experience for them.

After a very long three hours, we pulled in to their driveway, and I peeled myself out of my seat and opened the back door. I started to unbuckle Evan's seat belt and noticed a funny look on his face. He looked stoned. He hadn't slept during the ride—he had seemed overstimulated by the moon and the cars driving past us—so I blew it off, thinking it was exhaustion. I picked him up and brought him to the front door and put him on the ground. Grandma and Grandpa opened the door and got on their knees and devoured Evan with kisses. He wasn't responding at all, and he still looked stoned. I told Grandma I thought he was really tired, and if she wouldn't mind, would she get him in his PJs while I warmed up some milk. They whisked him into the bedroom as I warmed a bottle in the microwave. I remember hoping that Grandma and Grandpa wouldn't notice a big difference in his behavior. Since that first seizure, he hadn't been himself and now didn't even look like he remembered who they were. I didn't want their feelings to be hurt. They loved him so much.

WHEN THE BOTTLE was done, I walked to the back bedroom. As I passed through the door, I saw John holding Evan in his arms, and Grandma and Grandpa with looks of horror. John slowly laid Evan on the bed, and that was when I saw Evan's face. His eyes were dilated and rolled back and

13

to the side. It was happening again! Without saying anything, I leaped for the phone. I dialed 911 and was put on hold! I had forgotten we were in a city of older people who need to call 911 often. I was on hold for probably thirty seconds, but it felt like an eternity. I ran to Evan's side, and my heart sank. This didn't look like the previous seizure. It looked much worse. John was telling Evan over and over to stay with us, but it was clear that Evan was someplace else. After giving the operator the address, I hung up and started to examine what was going on. He was not convulsing this time and was not even trying to take in any air. The only thing coming out of his mouth was foam. I started to remove all of his clothing because I didn't know what else to do. I was screaming at everyone to put cold rags on him. Time was going by so slowly, and every second my heart was breaking. I couldn't believe this was happening to my baby again, and this time I knew it wasn't a febrile seizure. Something was terribly wrong. He was turning a pasty color, and there was still no sign of the paramedics. As more foam came out of his mouth, the pain in my heart was louder than words could describe.

"Where are those fucking paramedics?" I kept shouting.

Just as the paramedics pulled up, I saw my son go into cardiac arrest. I dropped to my knees and went numb. His eyes locked, and his whole body went limp. He lay there lifeless as the paramedics bolted through the door and checked for vital signs. They immediately started CPR. I knew they were shouting to each other, but I heard nothing except the sound of my heart beating and the thump of my tears hitting the carpet. As they continued with chest compressions, I asked God to talk to me, to tell me what was going on. I know we all come to this planet to learn lessons, but what the hell was I supposed to understand in this? Why was He taking my boy from me? I was a good person. I told God if He was taking Evan, he would have to take me, too. This boy was my everything, the sunshine in my life.

I leaned in to Evan's ear and whispered, "Evan, Mommy needs you here. It's not time. You come back and play with me some more, okay?"

God was talking, and I was listening.

I IMMEDIATELY FELT something come over my body. It was a wave of strength. I felt something tell my spirit he was going to pull through. It was saying, "Breathe, Jenny. Stay calm, he's coming back."

I don't know how, in the midst of the hell I was in, I managed to listen to such a statement as "stay calm," but I had no choice. My body relaxed, and the sounds of the room came back. I stood up and followed Evan into the ambulance. They made me sit up front, and I had to watch through a little window as they continued CPR. I kept telling myself, "He's going to be okay. He's going to be okay."

Finally, the paramedics stopped doing chest compressions and gave me the thumbs-up through the window. I burst into tears and put my head in my lap. Thank you, God. Thank you, God. Thank you, God.

The ambulance pulled away, and once again John was

following quickly behind. I was glad he had his mother and stepfather in the car with him. I couldn't even imagine what state of mind he might be in after witnessing what we just had.

As we pulled up to the ER, I jumped out of the passenger seat and ran to the back of the ambulance to greet Evan. I kept waiting for the medics to open the door and bring Evan out, and they weren't. I ran over to the driver to ask what the hell was going on, and he said he was seizing again. "Seizing again? What the fuck is going on?"

At last the back doors to the ambulance were thrown open, and Evan was out and we were running through the ER. The doctors quickly got the seizure to stop and stabilized him. Once again the barrage of questions began.

"Does epilepsy run in the family?"

"No."

"Did he have a fever?"

"No."

"Did he have a rash?"

"No."

"Did he have an injury?"

"No."

A doctor came and sat down with me and talked to me about seizures. He said that his own child had them every day and that I was lucky, because his child lived in a wheelchair and talked with a machine and Evan was healthy. I gave him a look that said, "That's supposed to make me feel better?" I climbed onto Evan's bed and lay next to him. The sound of the heart machine was music to my ears.

BEEP BEEP.

Thank you, God.

BEEP BEEP.

Thank you, God.

Again I started singing Evan's favorite lullaby.

John came into the room smelling like he had smoked a whole pack of cigarettes on the car ride over. John's mom and stepdad were there, too, but truthfully, I have no idea what they said or did, because all of my attention was on my little boy.

The doctor came back with more inconclusive test results and said that Evan would be better off in a hospital with more pediatric care. I couldn't agree more, but we were in Palm Springs, in the middle of the desert, and I didn't know how to get to L.A. safely. The doctors were already searching for a helicopter but were preparing an ambulance in case they couldn't get a helicopter in time. You can figure out what kind of condition your kid is in if they are taking him by helicopter from one hospital to the next.

While waiting for transportation, the doctors decided to give Evan an MRI, since the hospital we were being sent to would probably be very busy and we had a better shot of getting one done here. I agreed, and off Evan went for yet another test. I had no idea what they were looking for, other than a brain tumor that the CAT scan might have missed three weeks ago. The tests came back fine. No tumor or any other cause for concern. Evan had woken up for a moment, screamed something unintelligible, and was out again. At five A.M., it was time for us to head back to L.A. Sadly, the helicopter didn't make it in time, so we had to be transferred by ambulance. I sat in the back with Evan, with John following in the car. I looked at Evan, and stroked his head as we hit every pothole on the road, and sang him his tune.

The morning sun was rising, and the orange glow came through the windows. I looked straight into the sun and prayed. I prayed for a sunny day for my boy, filled with healing, answers, and peace. I knew I had no sleep in my future, but I didn't care if I ever slept again. I had a big job ahead of me. If the doctors weren't going to give me answers, I would find them myself.

Twenty minutes away from the Los Angeles hospital, I looked down and saw Evan's eyes open. I smiled at him, but my smile quickly faded. His eyes rolled back and to the left. "It's happening again! It's fucking happening again!"

One paramedic was driving, so I had to assist the one in back with me. I was turning buttons on machines, holding masks, and grabbing syringes. I was doing everything the paramedic was shouting at me to do. He injected Evan with Valium; my boy's eyes quickly shut, and his body relaxed. I collapsed on the floor of the ambulance and sat in silence until we reached the ER.

Once inside, we were bombarded by doctors. The medics filled them in on what had taken place, and from the looks on their faces, I could tell that they were confused. They all looked so young, just-got-out-of-high-school young. I asked them if they were doctors, and they said, "We're interns." Now, I know everyone needs to start somewhere, but I didn't want my son to be a pop quiz, so I asked them to bring in a neurologist as soon as possible. They ignored me and started with yet another barrage of questions.

"Did he have a fever?"

"No!"

"Is there any history of epilepsy in the family?"

"No!"

"Did he have any injury to the head?"

"No! No! No!"

I looked down at Evan and noticed his feet pointing straight and his fists locked in a tight grip. "Oh my God. I think he's seizing again!"

An intern leaped forward and confirmed what I had thought. She started using big fat medical words, and I started screaming, "Please don't let him go into cardiac arrest. Please just make these stop."

They immediately injected him with more Valium, and I thought, "How much Valium can a two-year-old take before he ODs?" Plus, they kept giving him Valium, and he continued to seize. Was that really the best thing for the job? I needed answers, and I wanted them *now*. "Can someone please get the pediatric neurologist in this room now?"

"We're completely qualified to take care of this situation," they replied.

I said, "I don't care if you won the fucking Nobel Peace Prize. I want someone with a degree in neurology who knows every part of the goddamn brain." They ignored me and began to tell me that they were going to take Evan for an

MRI. I replied, "Well, if you'd read the damn report I handed you when we got here, you would have seen we already had one!"

I know being a total bitch does not help any situation, but when your baby is sick, other people's stupidity is unacceptable. The interns looked confused again and walked out of the room. I lay down next to Evan and stared at his beautiful face. I stared at his chubby cheeks and his lips that looked just like mine and wondered what this journey meant for us. I knew I was a strong person, but my baby was going to have to be even tougher in the days ahead.

When the interns came back in the room, one of them said they wanted to test him for meningitis. I said, "You mean the test where you suck fluid out of his spine with a large needle?"

"Yes," she said.

"He just had one three weeks ago, so I really don't think he needs another one. It came back negative."

She replied, "Well, we need to test him again to rule out that he doesn't have it now."

"You've got to be kidding me."

I felt like everyone was looking in all the wrong directions. I've always had very good instincts, and I knew the interns weren't going to find anything. I argued with them for a bit more until they wore me down and I said yes. It was noon and I still hadn't slept. How could I?

I was still waiting for John to arrive from Palm Springs. I was so desperately craving a shoulder to lean on and couldn't understand what was taking him so long. I thought he had been following right behind the ambulance. At that very moment my two sisters, Joanne and Amy, walked in the door, and I wish I could say I broke down and held them, but I didn't. I simply stared at them, exhausted, and had no words to tell them about the last twenty-four hours.

I'm the oldest out of the three of us and always looked out for them. Growing up together, we used to play with our Cabbage Patch dolls and care for them as if they were our real babies. We would cut their hair and put makeup on their faces all the while knowing we would someday make the world's greatest mothers. Because neither of them had kids yet, I shared Evan with them. I would let them dress him up and smother him with love as if he were their own. Seeing them show up made me feel like my wingmen had arrived!

Amy commented on how sick I looked and said that she was very worried about me. She told me to get some shut-eye, but I told her it was impossible. Evan kept seizing, and I was the only one who seemed to notice. The nurse came in and said it would be at least another six hours before they did the meningitis test. My sisters begged me to lie down next to Evan; they said I looked like I was on the verge of passing out. The only reason I agreed was because they promised they would wake me up if they noticed any change in him. I had told them that if he clenched his fists so hard that they couldn't open them, he was seizing again. They understood, and I lay my head down on the pillow next to him. I took a big inhale and exhale and closed my eyes. Four minutes later my sister said, "Jenny, I think it's happening."

I bolted up and looked at his fists and started screaming

for the nurses. "It's happening again. Please, someone do something!"

The nurse ran in and injected him with more Valium. I screamed, "Why do you keep putting that shit in him? It only works for a short time. There has to be something better!"

It's amazing how easily medical staff ignores crying, yelling mothers. I understood they had to stay calm, but not on my clock, not while my kid could go into cardiac arrest. They were going to help.

His little fists relaxed again, and I knew that the seizure had stopped. I looked at Amy, who had tears in her eyes. I wished I, too, had the energy left to cry. I collapsed back onto Evan's pillow and fell asleep. I trusted my sisters could keep watch and decided to surrender to exhaustion. Less than fifteen minutes later, Amy said, "Jenny, it's happening again."

I bolted up and ran into the middle of the nurses' station and started screaming like Shirley MacLaine. "My son is seizing again! My son is seizing again! My son is seizing again! Do something to make these stop!"

"Ma'am, calm down," the nurse said. She ran into the room to inject him with—guess what? That's right, more Valium!

I screamed even louder. "My son has gone into cardiac arrest and has seized six fucking times today, and I still haven't seen one fucking neurologist! Not one fucking neurologist has come into this fucking room, and my son won't stop seizing! Find the fucking doctor! Go! Find the fucking doctor!"

I wish I could say that Evan didn't have any more seizures that night, but he did. I wish I could say that the neurologist showed up that night, but he never did. They kept injecting him and injecting him and injecting him. This was supposed to be a well-respected hospital and I felt like we were in a Third World country, being cared for by thirteen-year-olds.

I felt so hopeless and alone. I needed a partner in all of this, and my husband never showed up that night. I sat on Evan's bed. It was now midnight. Evan hadn't seized in two hours and had already been through the meningitis test, which, of course, came back negative. I stared out the window at all the cars going by. I wished to God that I could switch places with someone in one of those cars. I envied the people driving along, singing along to songs on the radio, enjoying life.

Chapter 3

‿

I STAYED UP ALL NIGHT, staring at Evan and waiting for any weird movements, but he didn't move. The seizures had stopped, or at least I thought they had stopped. He was so incredibly drugged up that I didn't know what to expect when he opened his eyes. I'd never heard of anyone seizing so often in one day. He had eight seizures that night, and I prayed that he would not have brain damage. More then anything in the world, I craved to hear "Mama" again.

Needless to say, the staff did not like me. When they came in to check on Evan, I could tell they were scared of me. That morning, whenever anyone walked in the room, I would say, "Did you find the neurologist yet? Is he coming?"

They didn't even have a response for me. I mean, really, let's stop for a moment to discuss the insanity of still not having seen the neurologist. I knew that the day before had been Easter, but I didn't want to believe that some asshole would rather stay seated at a dinner table with his ham and potatoes than come save my two-year-old. I just hoped to God he would show up very soon, otherwise holy hell was going to let loose.

Just as the sun started to shine through the blinds, I saw Evan's eyes slowly open. I was the only one in the room, and I leaned in toward him. "Hi, baby bird, it's mama bird."

He moaned for a bit, and I stroked his head. He looked very uncomfortable. It wasn't only that each arm had an IV in it, and he was attached to a heart monitor; his whole being looked sick. I couldn't even begin to imagine what it felt like to have endured the battle he had just gone through. I poured some apple juice in a baby bottle and put it in his mouth. I could see a gleam of happiness that his mama had read his mind, even though there was no physical reaction. I simply felt it like most mothers can.

The door pushed open, and a technician came in with a giant monitor on a cart. "We're going to give him an EEG," she said.

"I don't know what that is," I said.

She told me it was to monitor the brain activity to see where the seizures were coming from. I said, "So if he doesn't have a seizure in the time it takes to do this test, you won't be able to see which part of the brain the seizures are coming from?"

"That's right," she said.

"He stopped having seizures late last night. There haven't been any today. Why didn't you do this test yesterday, when he was having a seizure every hour?"

"The test wasn't ordered until this morning."

"Wow, you people are really smart around here, huh? I'm sure in the heart unit, you do EKGs on people after they're already dead to check out their heart activity."

She stared at me for a moment and began to set up the test. "We need to glue these electrodes all over Evan's head and have these wires come out of them and plug them into the computer."

I said, "How many of them?"

"About eighty," she said.

"Jesus Christ" was the only comment I could muster. This kid had been through so much. How was I going to let them put cement balls with wires attached to them all over his head? So I told the technician she wasn't going to do anything until someone got me a video with some dumb stuffed animal singing so I might be able to distract him. Evan still hadn't said anything to me yet, but I could tell he was alert.

Moments later, Barney the Dinosaur was playing, and Evan's eyes slowly went up to the screen. I nodded at the technician, and we began to stick the wires all over his head. Predictably, Evan started screaming and pulling them off. Thank God my sisters showed up; they immediately turned into the live version of *Sesame Street*. Evan couldn't smile, but at least now his attention was on them. The sight of my two sisters with big boobs dancing and singing rubber-ducky songs was good enough to make me crack half a smile.

Once the electrodes were in place, the technician made my sisters leave the room. They also told me not to talk to Evan or engage him because they needed him to relax. So I lay down next to him and watched his profile as he stared at the television. Thirty minutes went by very peacefully. Evan didn't squirm or move. He just looked comfortable watching Barney. The technician finally said, "We're done."

"Really? But he didn't have any seizures, so how will you ever know where they're coming from?"

She said, "Your son had three seizures in the past thirty minutes."

"What?" I said. "What the hell do you mean? He didn't tighten up. His eyes didn't roll back."

She said, "People can have seizures that don't cause any body movements at all."

"So my son is one giant walking seizure? He just keeps seizing and seizing?"

"I can't answer that question," she said. After a moment she said, "Can I ask you if he ever had an injury to the front of his head?" She pointed to his forehead.

"No! He was never dropped. He never ran into anything," I said.

"Some seizures that come from that area are caused by an injury to the brain," she said. With that, she left the room, and I felt even more confused. What did that mean? It still left me completely lost, and I was getting absolutely no answers. It was now noon the next day, and I still hadn't seen a neurologist.

My husband was nowhere to be seen. My sister JoJo said he was at home, making something for Evan. "Making something for Evan?" I said. "That's crazy. I haven't slept. I'm going through all of this on my own, and my husband hasn't set foot in this hospital yet. It's ridiculous."

A tray of juice and Jell-O came in, and I saw Evan moan for it. He still hadn't eaten in all of this time, and with the gallons of Valium running through his system from yesterday, I knew he would probably get sick. I sat him up and fed him some Jell-O. He swallowed it whole and screamed and kept opening his mouth for more. The nurse went and grabbed another one, and I fed it to him. Moments later, I laid him back down and saw a look on his face that said he was going to get sick. I knew he didn't have the energy to sit up and be sick, so I grabbed him and flung him over my shoulder, and he vomited. This went on all day with everything he put in his mouth. By that evening he had puked on me at least eleven times, until his body could hold down food.

It was dark outside when John finally walked in the door. The sight of me with no sleep and puke all over my body would have made most people say, "Oh my God, I'm so sorry I wasn't here to help you." He said he'd been busy at home all day, making a montage of video clips of Evan growing up. I couldn't really understand why. Maybe it was therapy for him. But I needed him to be at the hospital with me, and he wasn't. This was my first sign that I was embarking on this journey without my husband at my side.

John's parents had come, too, and my sisters still hadn't left my side. Moments later, guess who else finally walked in the door? That's right! The neurologist. It was eight P.M. and we had been in the hospital two whole days, and Dr. I Can Fix Any Brain Except My Own had just strolled in the door with a big smile. As a mother who had been to hell and back,

I couldn't decide whether to tear him a new asshole or bite my tongue so hard it bled, in order to get some help for my son.

He smiled at me and held out his hand. I paused for a moment and then shook it. "Hello, Doctor. It's so great to see you," I said in the nicest tone I could muster.

He asked to speak to John and me in the hallway, since the room was filled with visitors. As we walked down the hall, I kept hoping for an answer. I was praying to God for an explanation that made sense. We stopped and sat down, and the doctor looked at us and said, "Evan has epilepsy."

I sat back and felt relieved to have a label I could hold on to—something I could research and learn about. My relief lasted only a second, though. My emotional guidance system didn't agree. I blurted out, "That just doesn't seem right. Other doctors from the last hospital said that epilepsy usually runs on one side of the family. That's why everyone kept asking me that question over and over again. It feels like we're missing something." Honestly, it was my maternal gut instinct that epilepsy was not the end of this road. I felt like there was a highway ramp that everyone was not getting on. I had no other proof at this time to back this up, only a big fat voice screaming, "You're missing the bigger picture!"

"You're just having a tough time accepting it," the doctor said.

"No, sir, I'm not. In fact, I really hope it is epilepsy, because I will make sure to do everything I can so that he never again has another seizure."

The doctor said, "Has he ever had an injury to the front part of his head?"

No, I said. "Why does everyone keep asking me that?"

He went on to discuss different types of medicine that Evan would take to control his seizures. It would be kind of a scary game we'd have to play. Some worked on some kids, and some didn't. We had to hope we picked the right one so he didn't have to go through this anymore. The doctor sent us back to the room and said he was going to start Evan on what I'm going to call the blue seizure meds (and they were not actually blue) so I don't get sued.

So that night they injected Evan with the blue seizure meds, and I lay next to him and attempted to go to sleep for the first time in two days. John slept on the little cot in the room while I cuddled Evan, who tossed and turned and kicked and punched me in his sleep. I'd never seen him like this and thought maybe he was going through withdrawal from the large amount of Valium. I didn't sleep much that night, either, but I was becoming quite used to it by now.

The next morning, after we all woke up, John said he had to go home to take care of something. To this day, I still have no idea what he was going home to do. When he walked out of the room, I sat there pondering why my husband kept leaving me alone in the hospital. I know women are cut out to handle these types of situations better than men, but for God's sake, guys, don't abandon us because you can't deal. When I walked around the floor in the hospital, I noticed that it was mainly moms sitting with their sick babies. I wasn't the only one without a husband there.

Later that afternoon, the EEG technician came back to do the test again to see if the seizures had stopped now that

Evan was on seizure meds. We glued on the electrodes again. Thank God, the test showed no seizures—a small victory I felt deep in my soul. I still had no idea why all of this had happened in the first place, but at least my baby had stopped seizing.

It was now our fifth day in the hospital, and we were getting ready to be discharged. Evan didn't seem like himself yet; he couldn't stand up on his own without falling over. He seemed to have gone a little crazy since starting the blue meds, and I didn't know what to make of it. I was hoping his brain was trying to settle from the earthquakes it had just gone through, but I didn't know. I looked at the heart monitor he was hooked up to, and I badly wanted to shove it in my purse and take it home with me. It was comforting for me to hear the beep-beeps and know his little heart was doing its job. Unfortunately, the monitor wires were connected to the nurses' station, so stealing it was out of the question. Instead, I flipped it over and wrote down the name and planned on Googling it the moment I got home.

The nurses all waved goodbye, and out of the corner of my eye, I thought I saw a nurse give me the finger. That's all right by me. I was just looking out for my boy. I smiled and waved back and wished them well.

Driving home from the hospital should have been the most joyous occasion, but it wasn't. I was scared and completely exhausted. I did not have full-time nanny help because, like I said in my other books, I always did the majority of raising Evan. But now I prayed my husband would offer some relief. We didn't talk much on that car ride. "Have we run out of diapers yet?" was about the extent of it.

We pulled up in front of the house, and I wanted to feel like I was happy to be home. I wanted to feel like we were safe here, but I knew now that there was no safe place. That home was just another location where anything could happen.

Chapter 4

∽

IT WAS TURNING dark outside. It was time to give Evan his blue seizure meds for the first time at home. I injected the liquid into his mouth and forced him to swallow it. I could tell it didn't taste good, but I didn't care. I held his mouth shut until he swallowed all of it. I was not taking a chance of him missing even one drop.

That night I put him to bed and kissed him and told him I would be back in a few minutes. He wasn't responding to anything I had to say. I walked out of the room, watching him stare blankly at the ceiling. Most kids want to cuddle or read a book and don't want their mommies to leave them. Not Evan. He'd never cared when Mommy left his bedroom, ever. I always just thought he was being brave, but there was something different this time. He seemed to be not even present in his body. "Invasion of the body snatchers" would be the best way to put it. Evan was not Evan. I left his room and walked into my bedroom, where John was encouraging me to sleep in our bed. It was our first night back in the house, and I told him he couldn't pay me millions of dollars to be away from my child for longer then twenty minutes. Then he asked me to lie down with him because he wanted to have sex. We had just brought our kid home from the hospital, and he wanted sex! That's the difference between some men and women. We really do tend to handle stresses much differently, and I know deep down that John was trying to escape the only way he knew how—with sex—but I did not oblige.

I walked back into Evan's room and lay down next to him. He stared at the ceiling for the next three hours without saying a word. I wondered where my boy had gone. My eyes closed before his, and I drifted into a peaceful sleep.

WHACK! KICK! PUNCH!

I bolted out of the bed. I looked at Evan and saw that he looked almost possessed. He was yelling gibberish at me and violently flailing his arms and legs. I didn't understand what was going on. I said, "Evan, baby, what's wrong? It's Mama."

He kicked and screamed and shouted. John ran in the room to see what was going on. He started yelling at me, and I started yelling back at him while Evan was drowning out both of us with his screaming. John turned around and walked back into our room. I tried everything that night to get Evan to calm down.

When the sun was coming up and his little voice was cracking from screaming and fighting all night, he literally passed out in my arms on the floor, and I slumped back against the wall. It was six A.M., and I wish I could say he slept for a good eight hours, but he didn't. Two hours later, he woke up and the craziness continued.

John's mother and stepfather, Joyce and Roger, had decided to come over to help me out a bit. I was grateful because it meant I could catch maybe a full hour of sleep. It had been a week since that Easter night, and you can imagine how torn apart and exhausted I felt by this point. I didn't know what Joyce would think of Evan's behavior, because even I didn't recognize this child.

After a good three-hour nap, I woke up and stumbled into the living room. John's mom and stepdad were sitting on the couch watching Evan. The room was silent. Not at all what you would expect from grandparents visiting their grandson. It wasn't their fault, though. There was no communicating with Evan in this condition. I sat down, and we all stared at Evan spinning in circles. He would stop from time to time and run back and forth and flap his arms and then return to spinning. He wanted nothing to do with toys or people. He was in a world unto himself, and no one could do anything about it. John's mother asked, "Is this normal, dear?"

"I have no idea. I don't know who to ask anymore." I couldn't take the way everyone stared at Evan, so I brought him into the other room and played with him the best way I could. My heart was not just breaking at this point—it was destroyed.

I decided to call the company that made the heart monitors like the ones in the hospital and order one for Evan. I couldn't sleep at night, wondering if he was having a seizure that would lead to cardiac arrest, so I thought if I had an alarm that monitored his heart, I might be able to sleep again someday. When I called the company, they said it was for hospital use only, or by prescription from a doctor who had to state clearly that the child was in dire need. I called my pediatrician, and he attempted to tell me how he didn't think it was necessary. Before he could even get the word "necessary" out, I screamed, "You have no fucking idea what I have gone through in the past week. I need this goddamn machine, so fill out the fucking prescription and fax it to me now!"

As usual, there was silence for a brief moment, followed by: "Okay. I'll fax it right now."

I faxed it to the company, and they informed me that it would cost five thousand dollars. This was just the beginning of the enormous fees that would present themselves, but my spirit had no other choice. I said, "Yes, and could you please overnight it?"

That night I gave Evan more of the blue seizure meds and put him to bed. I lay next to him again, and about an hour later, WHACK, PUNCH, SMACK. Evan started to go berserk again. This time John's parents witnessed the whole ordeal. They looked sick as they watched Evan lose his mind. Again, I was up all night with him, until about six A.M. when John's mom took him from me and forced me to go to bed. God bless her.

Sadly, I had a dream that this was all a dream. I woke up feeling refreshed and thought it was a normal day. That lasted all of four seconds. Sadness came over my heart, and I walked back into the living room to see what this day had brought me. Evan was asleep on the sofa, and his grandma looked so worried that I had trouble looking at her. I knew that this was not Evan. Could it be the seizures that were causing him to be crazy? I didn't know where to turn. My husband was in the house but somehow managing to steer clear of me. I knew we just couldn't have a civilized conversation, so I kept searching for answers on my own.

That day the heart monitor showed up, and it was as if Ed McMahon were at my door with a giant check. I jumped up and down and was so excited to have the best security blanket money could buy. John was also excited because it meant he might get his wife back. The alarm portion of the heart monitor would be connected to our bed.

That night we hooked Evan up, and I felt so good knowing a deafening sound would alarm the house if his heart rate dropped or elevated at all. As usual, I gave him the blue seizure meds and put him to sleep. I plopped in my own bed for the first time and slept in my clothes, not because I needed to be dressed in case of an emergency but because it would prevent my husband from putting his penis anywhere near my skin. We weren't getting along, and as lonely as I felt, if the emotional component of the relationship wasn't there, I wasn't interested in sex.

BEEP BEEP BEEP BEEP!

The alarm was going off. I bolted into the room and saw that Evan had ripped the cords off and was on his hands and knees, slamming his head into the headboard.

BAM BAM BAM.

I screamed, "Stop it, Evan."

BAM BAM BAM.

I whisked him up and held him in my arms. He started wailing and speaking gibberish. He was banging his hand against his head over and over. John came in and started yelling at him to stop, and I started yelling at John that he didn't even know he was doing it.

"I think the seizure medication is making him psychotic," I said.

I begged Evan to calm down, but he kept hitting and kicking. I wrestled with him all night until we both collapsed on the floor at about six A.M. and fell asleep.

The next morning I called Evan's brain-dead neurologist and told him we needed to try a different medicine. I told him that this one was causing hallucinations and violent behavior and that last night he'd been trying to hurt himself. Of course, the doctor scoffed that this amazing medicine would cause any reaction like that, but I told him that ever since we had started giving it to Evan at the hospital, he'd been getting progressively more violent. The doctor told me I should stick with it. My emotional guidance system told me he was making another terrible mistake. Sometimes mothers instinctively know what works and what doesn't, but the doctor wasn't interested in hearing anything I had to say. I hung up and went online and did some research.

That next night, like clockwork, the same thing happened, but even worse than you could imagine. I ran into Evan's room, and this time he was hallucinating and batting things away from himself. He was screaming "Mama" but didn't recognize me. He was hitting me as if I were a stranger while screaming to find me. It was breaking my heart. I didn't know what to do, so I started screaming at the top of my lungs. John ran into the room, and I passed Evan over to him. I ran outside and screamed and wished that God would take it all away. I couldn't see my son in this kind of agony anymore. I asked God to take him if that meant he wouldn't suffer anymore, because I couldn't bear one more second of it. I cried and cried and then did what most mothers do. I wiped off my face and headed back into the house.

I picked up the phone and paged the neurologist. When he called me back at one A.M., I put the phone next to Evan and let the doctor hear the sounds this child was making, sounds that would make any person's soul go numb. "We're taking him off the blue medicine immediately," the neurologist said.

Sadly, he had refused to take my word for it. Evan had had to endure another horrific night for this idiot to see what the medicine did to him.

We switched to the next medicine, which I'll call the yellow seizure medicine (again, they were not actually yellow). I'm happy to report that the psychotic portion of Evan disappeared completely. He slept full nights on this new yellow medicine, which meant I finally slept, and he never again fought away invisible demons. But during the day, it was a different story. The yellow medicine caused him to lose all speech. Up to now he knew a handful of words, like "juice" or "mama." I wasn't getting that anymore. He also drooled and stayed locked in a daydream while staring at the wall. I called the doc and told him now I had Ozzy Osbourne for a child. I told the doctor that Evan had been a very happy boy who liked people, but now he was a zombie. The doc told me to hang in there, because it was a really good medicine. I got upset. I had no idea what this medicine felt like. It wasn't like I could ask Evan, so I decided to do what I'm sure many would say is a really dumb thing and take Evan's seizure meds to see how they made me feel. I needed to know if it was the medicine making him like this or something new. About an hour after taking the medicine, I swear to God, I could barely hold the saliva in my own mouth. My thoughts were confused, and I couldn't stop daydreaming.

I didn't know what to do. Did I take psycho kid, or did I take zombie kid? I settled for zombie kid until I was able to figure out some more on my own.

Chapter 5

∾

Searching for a Miracle

AS THE WEEKS went by, my Mommy and Me group called me again and again to try to set up something with the old playgroup gang. I couldn't bear to have them see my son like this. I kept turning them down and allowed in only close family, and even that was difficult. My sisters looking at Evan with sad eyes made me want to keep everyone away.

Being raised Catholic, my mother had contacted pretty much every church or living saint on earth to pray for a blessing. I received cards, prayer cards, angel statues, rosaries, and holy water from Madjagoria that I put on Evan every night. I contacted an Indian sweat lodge I used to go to and asked them to pray for Evan in all of their ceremonies. I had overheard someone talking about the Mormons having some amazing healing prayer that cured people. A close friend of mine told me that was how they'd brought their child out of a coma, and yada yada yada. Now, I'm a pretty grounded person and don't believe everything I hear, but when you have a sick kid, you would cut off a chicken's head if you thought it would cure him. I'm sure it doesn't surprise anyone who has gotten to know me through my other books that I had the balls to contact the Mormon Tabernacle Church myself. I spoke to a man there and told them of my situation. I told them I was not a Mormon but would be so grateful if they could come and do this prayer for my son. They were very polite and agreed to send over the missionaries who had been "blessed," or whatever, to do it. I was so happy when I hung up, I called my mom and said, "Mom, the Mormons are coming over! The Mormons are coming over!"

She was happy for me mainly because it was the first time I had been able to get happy about anything in a very long time. Go figure!

So the day of the Mormons' visit arrived, and I was anxiously waiting. I cleaned the house and put Evan in a respectable outfit instead of his usual T-shirts with rock bands on them. I even made oatmeal cookies to give the Mormons as a thank-you, because I wasn't sure if they would be offended by money. John informed me that the Mormons had some pretty strict rules on swearing and sex and anything lewd. I replied, "Shit, I hope they don't fucking recognize me."

DING-DONG.

I ran and put on a sweatshirt to try and conceal any part of me that could possibly have a sexy curve, and then I answered the door. "Hello," I said.

My excited smile turned into an inquisitive one. The two men who were standing at my door and were able to perform miracles through their prayer were only about nineteen years old. As expected, they were wearing their long-sleeved white shirts and their long ties, and they looked very sweet. I invited them in and brought Evan over to greet them. They were very kind to him, and one of them even pulled out two small toy balls for him. Sadly, my son was still in zombie mode and didn't respond to them at all. They kept waving the balls around his eyes to get his attention, until I blurted out, "Evan, don't you want to touch this man's balls?"

Everybody fell silent. I could not believe what I had just said in front of the Mormons!

I looked at their faces and saw one of the boy's lips starting to quiver, and I burst out laughing. I laughed so hard I had tears coming down my face. At this point I didn't even care if I made them upset, because I needed this laugh more than anything. John watched his wife completely lose the grace she had tried to fake in the past ten minutes. After I wiped the tears away from my eyes, I apologized and asked them what we needed to do to prep for the prayer. They said to have Evan sit by himself in a chair. They were going to place their hands on top of his head and do a fifteen-minute prayer blessing. I said, "Evan doesn't like to be touched on the head at all, so the likelihood of you guys getting four hands to rest on his head for more than one second will be a miracle unto itself."

They kind of ignored my warning with, I must say, dignified confidence, and started the process. I sat Evan on the chair, and they placed all four hands on top of his head and I squinted, waiting to hear a smack and a scream come from Evan. Weirdly enough, I didn't hear a peep. Evan sat there while the Mormons did their thing, and I was amazed. I thought if they could get him to do that, maybe they could cure him from epilepsy. When the prayer was finished they removed their hands and told me they saw him healing in a year's time. I thanked them over and over again and ran into the kitchen to give them my homemade oatmeal cookies. They smiled and stood there staring at me while holding the plate of cookies. I smiled back, and we stood there in a moment of uncomfortable silence, all staring at one another. I couldn't figure out if this was a Mormon thing or if they wanted money or if they were going to lecture me on the whole "balls" comment.

Finally, I blurted out, "Um, can I make a donation to the church to say thank you?"

"No," they replied, and continued to stare at me. I then said, "Um, is there anything else I could do for the church, like more baked goods?"

I was hoping now to get them to go. One said, "We would appreciate you taking twenty minutes to sit down sometime and let us tell you about our church."

Oh! Now I understood what was going on. They were doing their sales thing. I told them I would love to do that at some other time, but right now my head was so caught up with healing my son, I couldn't possibly give them the proper attention. They said they understood and wanted to know when exactly they could come back. You gotta give those Mormons some credit. They know how to get things done. I told them to try back in a month or so.

With that, I went to give one of the boys a hug, and they kind of panicked and pushed away. All I could think of was how many rules I had broken in the thirty minutes they were already here. I would not make a good Mormon. I closed the door and watched them walk down my driveway in their white shirts, Bibles in hand.

These were just two of the many different healers I brought into Evan's life. I wondered what the neighbors must have thought, seeing every religion and cosmic being enter my house over the next few months. I didn't care. Whatever it takes, right?

The next week we were due for our follow-up visit with the brain-dead neurologist. I asked John to come with me because Evan was rough for me to handle on my own in public. I needed help, and that was that. We got to the office, and as expected, we waited four hours to see this doctor in whom I had so little confidence. John and I fought horribly the whole time. I yelled at him through clenched teeth to make our fighting a little quieter because the waiting room was completely full. I basically told him it was bullshit that he had spent so little time at the hospital. He fought back with his side of the story. I knew he'd been scared out of his mind, seeing Evan so sick in the hospital, but I had been, too, and I'd managed to be there. I had so much built-up resentment that I looked at him and said, "I want you to move out."

He looked at me in shock and then started yelling more. Evan started crying, and then I started crying, and then John stood up and left. At that moment they called Evan's name, and I scooped him up and walked down the hallway. Weirdly, I felt relieved and at peace. It was another emotional guidance system letting me know that I had made the right choice. Now I had to follow through and in fact make him move out.

As I walked down the hallway, I saw children with severe brain problems. Each child I saw brought tears to my eyes. I cried because I felt bad for them and their parents and because I was so grateful Evan was not as sick. Comparing your child to someone who has it worse makes you feel better. Sad but true.

We sat in a little office until the neurologist walked in the door and said, "How's everything going?"

"I don't understand the question," I said.

He looked at me and knew he wasn't going to get away with much fluff, so he got right to it. He talked about how the medicine would not affect Evan like this much longer, maybe a couple of months as his body got used to it. I looked down at Evan; the whole time the doctor was talking, Evan kept spinning in circles and flapping his arms. I interrupted the doctor to say, "Is this normal?"

"Is what normal?" he said.

"The flapping with his hands and spinning. He's always done it, but ever since his first seizure, it seems like it's all day long. Does it mean anything?"

"No, it's fine. Completely normal," he said.

"Really? I just feel like we might be missing something. It's a gut instinct. I just don't know."

He looked down at Evan and replied, "He looks great to me." And with that, he handed me a refill of the zombie drug, and I packed Evan up and we went home.

As you know, in life, when it rains, it pours. With Evan still sick and the fighting still going on with John, I had hoped to see a glimmer of something good in our future, but I wasn't so lucky. I received a call from the television producers I was working with, and they told me that the sitcom pilot I had shot as a possible series had not gotten picked up. The last thing I wanted to do was go back to work, but I was the main breadwinner in the family. There wasn't that much of a nest egg, and the pressure was always on me to pull us through to the next month.

In the meantime, my mother had started sending me everything she could find on epilepsy. I had bought some books on it myself but couldn't read them, for some reason. I wasn't in denial or anything; the books just did not resonate with me. I started to get frustrated and began my first step toward endless hours of research that would become my new full-time job. I looked at the EEG report and noticed that Evan's seizures were coming from the F4 lobe (his forehead). I went online to check out this lobe and found that most epilepsy seizures come from the temporal lobe, which is the soft spot on your temple. I was dumbfounded. I read further on and saw that frontal lobe seizures are sometimes caused by an injury to the brain.

Injury to the brain? That was why they kept asking me in the hospital if he'd ever had an injury to the head. How had Evan gotten an injury to the brain? And why hadn't they looked into *why* the seizures were coming from this lobe?

I slumped back in my chair and prayed to God He would point me in the right direction. I prayed He would hand-deliver me a person who could say, "Here you go, Jenny. Here is a doctor who knows all the answers."

Chapter 6

∽

God's Connections

THE NEXT DAY I woke up and fired my agent, whom I actually adored, but I needed a fresh start and an agency that was excited to have me. I desperately needed to get my ass out there working again. I took a meeting that week with a new agency and somehow managed to throw on lip gloss and a smile and walk in the door. It was nice to see faces that were thrilled to see me instead of all the worried, sad people who now populated my life. In the meeting, I talked about how I planned to take over Hollywood and blah blah blah. I did anything I could to show that I was a chick willing to work. I was going on and on and was surprised at how well I was faking happiness until someone asked me about Evan. I've never been a good liar, as you can tell from all of my books, so I had no choice but to blurt out, "Well, he's been really sick."

"Oh no," they all replied.

I told them the edited version of the past couple months, and the president of the company said, "Hey, I can get you in to see the top neurologist in the world, if you'd like."

At the very moment I think angels started doing dances all around the room, and "Hallelujah" was faintly heard being sung all the way from heaven. THANK YOU, GOD!

I looked at him with big doey eyes and replied, "Yes, yes, I would love my boy to see the best neurologist in the world. I would love nothing more in the world, actually." With that, the agent popped open his phone and got me in the next day, when it normally would have taken three months. I knew God had just answered my prayers, and I was so grateful that I never had to see that horrible brain-dead neurologist again!

I had to shoot a *For Him Magazine* layout the next day but begged the editor to shoot my photos as fast as he could so I could make a very important doctor's appointment. They agreed, and I bent over and gave them the best cleavage shots ever just to get the fuck out of there. The whole time I stood there in these sexy poses, I kept thinking: "If only people knew how incredibly sad I am about my sick boy, they would think I am the best actress in the world." You never would have been able to tell from those pictures. Moms gotta do what moms gotta do.

As soon as the photographer yelled, "It's a wrap," I flung off my bikini and threw on sweats and raced down to the doctor's office with Evan. Once inside, John and I sat there and didn't talk to each other. He knew I still wanted him to move out, and he was avoiding confrontation. I hoped that this was the doctor I had prayed for—someone who actually knew what the hell he was talking about. My instincts had always been right about people, and if this guy turned out to be a bozo like the last one, I didn't know what I would do to the medical community. My heart was beating so fast, Evan probably thought it was a drum beating in the next room. As happy as I was to be there, I was terrified to hear more bad news. In my dream of dreams, I was hoping the doc would say, "Because you pushed for three hours and he was stuck in your canal and had to be born by C-section, it caused some damage in the frontal lobe." In my mind, that was the best-case scenario.

The door opened, and a sweet, older-looking man walked in the door. He greeted all of us, and I immediately felt good about him. I started telling him about all the seizure activity that had taken place and what had been said so far. He listened closely but had his eyes on Evan the whole time. I could tell he was evaluating Evan's bizarre behavior. He asked me a couple of questions and seemed very peaceful about the whole thing. I was starting to feel more and more relaxed as he played with Evan. Then he stood up and opened his office door and told his secretary to cancel his next appointment. I thought to myself, "Wow, he must really like us. This is some big VIP treatment." He closed the door and pulled his chair up close to mine and put his hand on my hand. He looked at me with sorrowful eyes and said, "I'm sorry, your son has autism."

Chapter 7

∽

"I'm sorry, your son has autism."

I CLOSED MY EYES.

"It's a beautiful boy!"

I teared up as they handed me the most amazing creation I had ever seen. I looked down at those little blinking eyes and started crying so hard at the beauty that God had helped me make. At that moment I had an overwhelming feeling that I had given birth to a child who was going to make a difference in this world. I even looked at the nurses with amazement and told them about my overwhelming feeling. They looked at me kind of like "Yeah, yeah," but I didn't care. I knew someday they would see what I had seen in this new little spirit. I looked down at my boy and whispered, "You're going to be glad you picked me. I'm going to be the best mom in the world, and I'm gonna do everything in my power to make the world a better place and not let anything harm you."

With that, they whisked him out of my arms to begin his welcome-to-this-planet party, consisting of tests and injections.

Looking back, I can see that little signs presented themselves here and there, but as a loving mother who wanted to see only the good, I looked past most of the red flags along the way. My friends' babies had all cracked a smile way before Evan did, but I knew babies do things on their own clock and not to compare. When I put Evan in a Halloween costume and plopped him up against a chair, even though he had no idea he looked like a pea in the pod, I did, and it made me laugh so hard. That was the moment I saw his first half of a smile. I stopped midlaugh to stare at the rainbow on his face. He was almost five months old, and I ran outside and started doing a happy dance and yelling in the neighborhood, "My boy just had his first smile, and it was because of *me*. I made him laugh." As an actress, I work so hard to make people laugh, but this was the smile that would stay with me forever.

Though Evan continued to hit all of his milestones, I can see things now that stuck out slightly. They were never that obvious to me until now.

In playgroups, he was the boy who never took anything away from other kids. I would constantly watch little baby bullies come over to Evan and whisk his ducky away from him. Most kids would cry and scream, "I want my ducky back." Evan didn't. He just sat there, not even really knowing that the ducky was gone. I would always get up and replace it with another toy. I remember thinking, "Look how sweet my little angel is, he didn't even mind that his toy was ripped out of his hands." As he got a little bit older, we would go out with a friend of mine who had a child about nine months older. Her kid seemed so hyperactive. We would be sitting in a restaurant, and this kid could not sit still no matter how hard his mom tried, whereas Evan would play peacefully with a straw for two hours. It wasn't until later that I realized the other kid was normal. It was not quite normal that my boy could flick a straw over and over and over for hours on end and be totally into it.

When it came time to start saying his first words, he said "Dada" when all of his friends did. I was kind of disappointed that it took him four more months to say "Mama," but it was well worth the wait. Just before he started walking, he would rub his feet together like a cricket when he got excited. I would always laugh and say, "Oh, look at the cricket rub his feet together when he gets so happy." A couple of months later, when he was able to stand, I noticed that because he was standing on his feet, unable to do cricket feet when he got excited, his hands would flap like a butterfly or a bird. That was when I started to call him my little bird. I thought it was so cute, and I found it kind of interesting that this trait had transferred from his feet to his hands. Wherever we would go, people would comment on it, and I would giggle and say, "Yep, he's gonna fly south for the winter at any moment now."

I had no idea flapping was a common characteristic of

autism. Tiptoe walking and spinning in circles all day are two more that are high up on the list. You would have thought his pediatrician might have noticed something along the way, mind you, but he did not. At one appointment he asked me if Evan was saying anything, and I said yes, because he was speaking a few words. That was the extent of my pediatrician checking for delays.

I also remember looking in Evan's playroom and noticing that I had bought him a ridiculous number of toys that were always untouched. Anytime I gave him a new toy, he wouldn't truly play with it. I thought he was finicky. Little did I know it was because he had no idea *how* to play with toys. He would play with only cause-and-effect toys, like a tube that made a funny squeak noise after being picked up. He would turn the miniature monster trucks upside down and spin the wheels for hours. The trucks never went "vroom vroom." He was addicted to the motion of the spinning wheel. For the first two years, I was the main person who played with Evan. I always had a hard time, but I thought it was because he was too young to play hide-and-seek, and I didn't know anything else to do besides tickle him, sing songs, or read books. Now I know it wasn't my fault. I tried, but he wasn't interested.

If I ever left him alone in the playroom, I would come back and find him playing with the oddest things. He had such a fascination with door hinges. They excited him so much that I finally let him play with them, but he would do it all day if I let him. I honestly thought and told people he was going to be a mechanic when he grew up. He loved springs and shapes and gears. I didn't see anything wrong with it.

As time went on, I noticed that when we went to other people's houses for Mommy and Me playdates, their playrooms were filled with more advanced toys—airplanes and LEGOs and action figures from television. I shouldn't say "advanced." They were actually typical for their ages, but to me, they seemed advanced. Evan's playroom still had only baby toys lying around, even though he was two years old. They were all Evan wanted to play with, besides door hinges. Now, I don't want people to think I'm a total idiot for not seeing any signs in that. I really didn't because when I had playdates at my house those same kids would play with the baby squeak toys. I figured in due time, Evan would like other toys, but I wasn't going to force him into it.

A close friend of mine once had made a comment about the DVDs I would put on for all the kids to watch. She wanted to know why I was still putting on the infant Baby Einstein. I said, "Because it's Evan's favorite." He had turned two and a half, and I guess all his friends were watching *Bob the Builder*. I remember thinking, "Evan would never be interested in that, since there's a complicated story, and he would be so bored." He just liked to watch objects spin and those puppet animals that don't talk. If I'd had an older child, I might have picked up on some of these signs quicker, but I'm sure most mothers of autistic children would tell you that nothing seemed like that big a deal . . . yet.

When the playgroup met at the mall, we would take our kids to those germ-infested toy areas where our children could play inside. Every single time we went, my friends' kids would be climbing the plastic turtles while Evan and I had to ride the escalators about a hundred times. I'm not exaggerating. Up down, up down, up down. I would wave to all my friends each week as they laughed at me riding the escalator over and over and over. After we got off the escalator, we also had to watch it for at least twenty minutes because Evan was so mesmerized by those simple moving stairs. All he would say was "Escalator, escalator, escalator, escalator, escalator, escalator, escalator," then flap his hands. I was thinking my kid was going to be an engineer for sure! Eventually, riding the escalator became an addiction for Evan. He never wanted to go to the park or Disneyland. He just wanted to ride the damn escalator, and because I didn't know how to play with him at home and wanted to see him happy, I brought him to the mall almost every day.

In terms of speech development, Evan did not stick out like a sore thumb. He had some words, such as "juice" or "cookie," and my friends were amazed by the fact that he could sing an entire Dave Matthews song and not miss a word. I'd always thought autistic kids couldn't talk at all, so no bell went off in my head. I know this sounds strange, but I thought I had given birth to somewhat of a genius. I thought that because he wasn't into toys; he was smart; and even though other kids were saying full sentences, my kid could recite an entire book that was closed because he had it memorized. For some reason, autistic children have amazing memories. I knew Evan had no idea what any of the words meant. Words were just sounds, and if he ever heard things more than a few times—like a song or a book—he seemed to connect to the rhythm of the words and would recite them back. He had very little "original" speech. He could not formulate his own ideas. He would simply memorize and repeat.

I remember going to the grocery store and seeing the issue of *Time* magazine about autism and buying it. I got home and read it and thought, "Thank God my kid does not have autism." To me, autism was a closed-off child who allowed no one inside. Evan loved me, and he smiled, even though I did have to work a little harder for it. As he got older, people started to suggest that something was a bit off. Needless to say, being the proud mother I am, I could not disagree with them more and made sure they knew it.

The first mention came from my mother-in-law. Every cliché in the book will tell you that no criticism should ever come from your mother-in-law, because it always feels like she's telling you that you're doing things wrong even though she's actually trying to help. I was at work, shooting some TV show that I'm sure was cheesy, and the sitter whom I used when I worked was watching Evan. My mother-in-law was in town, staying with me, but I still thought it was a good idea to have someone around who knew his daily needs. They were both sitting in the playroom, watching Evan, and my mother-in-law said to the sitter, "Do you notice Evan not being affectionate toward people? He seems very aloof and not welcoming to me. I think Jenny lets him watch too much TV."

My sitter looked at her and was immediately offended.

This girl loved Evan as much as I did and could not believe anyone would say that. "He is *very* affectionate and radiates love for every person who comes in contact with him. He is the sweetest child, he never gets upset or yells, and you couldn't be more wrong—he barely watches any TV!"

When I got home from work, my mother-in-law was not there, so my sitter filled me in. I was enraged that my mother-in-law had accused Evan of not being loving. I nearly had a nervous breakdown in the house. To me, Evan was perfect, and anyone who had a problem with that had some serious issues. When my mother-in-law came back, I got in a huge fight with her. When she left to go back home, I wrote her a letter explaining how wrong she was. I now know I was incredibly in denial. Sadly, my mother-in-law got the first lashing. Not even one drop sank into my head. She would not be the last to mention something was wrong.

The next messenger who crossed my path was at a play gym: a woman who worked in the painting section, helping the kids make pictures. Evan was painting and flapping his arms because of all the pretty colors everywhere. I was sitting with all of the other mommies, gossiping, when this woman came over and gently asked me if my son had a mental problem. I was in shock that, first, anyone could ever say anything like that, and second, say anything about sweet flapping Evan. I screamed no to her and told management that one of their employees basically had asked if my child was retarded. She was let go the next week. Needless to say, I now feel really bad about it, but at that time, her remark was like a punch in the stomach.

Finally, it was time to put Evan into preschool. I went with him to his new Montessori school and got to hang with him on the first day. There were five-year-olds mixed with the two-year-olds because that was the way this school did it. The older kids looked like high school kids next to Evan, and I was a bit worried about how he would do in an integrated class. We were all sitting around with our kids when this little brat with piggy tails came right up to Evan's face and started screaming at him. She was nose to nose with him, and he didn't even see her or react. I remember thinking, "That's odd. Why wouldn't he react to this?" I wanted him to smack her away or do something, but he did nothing. He just looked straight ahead, almost as if he were deaf to her.

Three days later, I went to pick him up from school. It was recess, and they were all playing outside. I decided to eavesdrop and watch him play. He walked over to the slide, and a big five-year-old bully pushed him onto the ground. Normally, I would have gone over there and said some angry things to that five-year-old about how the Easter Bunny was coming to take his toys away, but I didn't. I forced myself to hang back. Evan lay on the ground. I knew he wasn't hurt, because he'd landed on a pile of leaves. He just lay there and stared at the sky. Most kids would have started crying and somehow mumbled to the teacher what the bully had done. Not Evan; he peacefully lay there, enjoying the clouds.

You would have thought that by now I might have said, "Hmmm, that's odd." Nope. Instead, I said to myself that Evan needed to go to a different school with kids his age so he wouldn't get bullied. I pulled him out of that school and signed him up at another one. He was to start at the new school the following week, but because I wasn't paying attention to all the signs God was giving me, He had to wake me up with a big one. The following week was when I found Evan seizing and struggling to breathe in his crib. And from that moment on, I was painfully awake.

Chapter 8

∾

I Opened My Eyes

"I'M SORRY, your son has autism."

"I'm sorry, your son has autism."

I stared at the doctor while remembering all the signs that had led up to this moment. I felt each membrane and vein in my heart shattering into a million pieces. Nothing had prepared me for this. I couldn't breathe. I wanted it gone. I had been through so much, with seizures and psychotic reactions to meds, I couldn't believe God had handed me another plate of shit. I still did not want to believe the doctor, even though this time my emotional guidance system was telling me he was right. I looked at the doctor with pleading tearful eyes. "This can't be. He is very loving and sweet and not anything like Rain Man."

"Every child is different," he said. "Some aren't as severe as others."

Jenny McCarthy

"I don't understand. How can this be? How can you tell after only a few minutes?"

He looked at me and then pointed to the corner. Evan had taken those ear cones the doctors use to look inside your ears and had made the most perfect row lined up across the room.

"Does he line up toys at home instead of play with them?" the doctor asked.

"Yes, but don't all kids do that?"

"Nope, not all," he said. "And they all don't flap like that, either."

I looked at Evan and saw that he was flapping his wings. I said, "Oh no, he just does that when he gets excited."

"That is called a stim," he said.

"A what?"

"A stim. A self-stimulatory behavior. It's an autistic trait."

I looked at Evan and saw him flapping, and once again had my heart shattered. I had always looked at it like an adorable Evan characteristic that was so cute and unique. I felt almost betrayed, as if I didn't know this child standing in front of me. Everything I had thought was cute was a sign of autism. I felt tricked. I guess the doctor got this from me because he turned my head back toward him and said, "He is still the same boy you came in here with."

No, in my eyes he wasn't. This was not Evan. Evan was locked inside this label, and I didn't know if I would ever get to know who he really was. The things I'd thought were personality traits were in fact autism characteristics, and that was all I had. Where was my son, and how the hell did I get him out?

66

John had started asking more questions, but all I heard was "WAWAWAWAWAWA." I went numb and stared across the room at Evan. At that moment I hated everything and everyone. I'd thought Evan was born to change the world, but how could he do that when he was locked inside a world of his own, one I didn't know if he would ever come out of? I kept thinking, "God, what am I supposed to do with this?"

The doctor put his hand on mine and snapped me back into the room. He said, "I'm taking Evan off the seizure meds he is on right now, and he's going to begin taking these new white pills very slowly. You can only increase dosage a little bit each week, because otherwise, he could get a fatal rash. Once he is at the proper dosage to stop his seizures, we will stop increasing."

"I'm sorry , did you say 'fatal'?"

"It's not going to happen, because we are going to increase the dosage slowly, but I need you to trust me that this is one of the best seizure meds for Evan. It has the fewest side effects."

"Wow, so not only will I be checking to see if he's breathing at night, I'll be doing a full skin exam to make sure a fatal rash doesn't show up, too?"

The doctor said, "You need to relax and trust me."

I did trust him. My motherly gut said, "Trust this man," so I planned on doing everything he said. It still didn't take away my fear of life's last-minute surprises that keep showing up. The doctor then told me he would hand me off to his protégée; being the number one neurologist in the world, he was a tad busy. He said the new neurologist dealt mainly with autistic children, and it would be a good fit.

God, hearing him say "autistic children" and the part about Evan being a good fit fucking killed me. I wanted to scream, "No, that's not a good fit! A good fit would be Evan being part of the 'too tall for his age' group. That's a good fit. I knew the doctor had the best intentions. I was still trying to scrape myself off the floor from all of this.

"Why do autism and seizures sometimes go together?" I asked.

"About thirty percent of children with autism suffer from seizures," he replied.

"I don't understand how 'no one' knows why autism is such an epidemic. That seems like bullshit to me." My heart cried as I finally let it sink in. My son has just been diagnosed with autism at two and a half years old. I started to get angry, but John had started the goodbyes, since he saw where I was about to take the conversation. The doctor gave me a hug, and we headed into the elevator. John looked at me and said, "How you doin'?" I shook my head, unable to speak. I was in too much pain to cry.

Once in the car, I reached down for my purse and opened a prescription for Ativan, which is like Valium, and popped two of them in my mouth. I needed to escape the pain as fast as I possibly could, before it got deeper into my soul. I put my head back and stared out the window, waiting for the beauty of legal narcotics to take my pain away. I looked at John and said, "I think we're going to have to put off your moving out. Let's try and make it work. I can't go through this alone."

Chapter 9

~

WE PULLED UP in front of the house, and I asked John to take Evan inside. I ran into the bedroom to call my mom. I wanted this phone call to be quick and to the point. I didn't want to hear my mother cry, because I could barely keep it together myself.

"Hello?" my mom said.

"Evan has autism."

"What?"

"Yep, and you're gonna have to call Amy and Joanne, because I can't say the word 'autism' anymore."

"Oh no, Jenny," she said with a heart-shattering quiver.

"I have to go lie down, Mom. I'll call you later." I hung up, plopped on my bed, and cried. I didn't feel like hearing my mom cry, which was why I'd gotten off the phone as quickly as possible. Sympathy and tears were the last things I wanted to hear at that moment.

Sadly, I couldn't lie in my bed and cry for weeks, like I

had hoped. Instead, if you can believe this, I had to somehow roll off my mattress and pack a very large suitcase. In a few hours, I had to leave for New York to do every talk show on TV to promote my second book, *Baby Laughs*. Yes, I had to somehow get ready to do an entire week of comedy about my baby, to sell this book so I could make a living to pay for autism. I don't think anybody in the world would have been able to get on a plane and do what I was about to do after finding out her child was autistic.

As I threw dresses and heels into my suitcase, I couldn't believe how shitty my life was. I know people like to think celebrities are immune from problems and have it so easy. Well, we don't. Here's your proof: We all suffer like everyone else. Don't let designer shoes fool you.

I reminded John exactly what to do and look for as far as fatal rashes were concerned and I begged him to give Evan as much attention as possible. I was also leaving a nanny in charge, but I wanted Evan to feel like a parent was still there. So I pleaded with John not to disappear inside the house.

As I stood there with my luggage, waiting to leave, I stared at Evan. How could God make me leave my child right then? I knelt down and told him I loved him and that Mommy would be back. As usual, he didn't react much to my leaving, but now I knew it wasn't because he was a strong, confident little boy who was so good, it was because autism made him not care that Mommy was leaving. I kissed him with tears and headed for New York.

∽

"HI, JENNY, your dressing room is right this way," the producer of *Live with Regis and Kelly* said with excitement. I walked down the hallway past smiling people who were excited to see me and more excited to see how goofy and funny I would be on the show.

"I think you're hilarious," one of the stagehands said.

I mustered up a laugh and put my head down so I didn't have to talk to anyone else on the long trip to my dressing room. I sat down, and the producer prepped me on the things Regis and Kelly would ask me, and I smiled and nodded. She wanted me to tell as many funny Evan stories as I could think of that people could relate to. I smiled and said, "No problem." But inside, I wanted to scream: "No no nooooooo. I don't want to talk about my baby!"

She left the room, and I looked up at the television screen. The show was beginning, and tears filled my eyes. "Today's guests on *Live* are so-and-so from *Desperate Housewives*, talking about something; Jenny McCarthy, promoting her new book, *Baby Laughs*; and Charlie Weis, the Notre Dame coach, talking about his new autism foundation, Hannah & Friends.

"Autism foundation?" I blurted out in my dressing room.

I opened the door to my dressing room and started wandering the hallways, looking for this man. I didn't want one soul to know about my son, but I thought this could be a message from God. I mean, think of the coincidence! I walked into the greenroom and saw him there with a lot of people. I asked him to join me in the hallway for a moment, and he got up and approached me. I took him around a corner and looked up at this sweet man, and with a quivering lip, I mumbled, "I just found out my son is autistic." And then I started to cry uncontrollably. He hugged me before he even had a chance to speak, because he saw the pain pouring out of me.

"Listen, there is so much help out there. You're not alone," he said. He went on to tell me about his child and all of the help they'd gotten, but I couldn't quite comprehend what he was saying. I think what I needed was the hug and someone else in the world who could relate to the pain I was in at that very moment. He took down my e-mail address and told me we would get in touch later, and he would help me out.

"JENNY, YOU'RE UP NEXT," the stagehand shouted to me. Charlie hugged me again, and I walked away quickly trying to wipe off any tear marks. They rushed me backstage and placed me on the mark where I had to wait for my name to be called. I looked into the little backstage mirror for celebrities to check their makeup and didn't recognize myself. I closed my eyes and prayed to my dead grandpa to come through me and be funny. He was the one who was the ham in the family, and I know I got it from him. "Grandpa, please, please help me. Help me get through this. Help me not to break down crying on live TV in front of millions of people. Help me sell this book so I can get another book deal so I can pay for all my bills. Help me help me help me."

"Please welcome *New York Times* best-selling author and very funny lady Jenny McCarthy," said Regis.

I took a big inhale and exhale and walked out into the lights. I smiled the biggest smile, waved to the audience, kissed Regis and Kelly, and sat down.

"So, how's your baby boy doing?" Kelly said gleefully. Oh my God, I couldn't believe that was the first question out of the gate. Even though I had become personal friends with Kelly, she had no idea what was going on, and since I was promoting a baby book, that question was a pretty good choice. It still made me want to start crying on her shoulder and sob about how much pain I was in, but I couldn't. I shoved the pain way deep inside the inner core of my bones and replied, "Great! Really great!" I immediately went into a joke and got the audience to laugh. "Okay, one joke down," I thought. "Can I get another?" I started to talk about my husband and how I'd neglected sex with him after having the baby and how he had the worse case of blue balls imaginable. The whole audience broke into laughter, and I didn't realize I had been censor-bleeped until Regis and Kelly had their hands over their mouth.

"Sorry, I didn't know that was a bad thing to say." I said. I was hoping to make sense at this point, not caring what was or wasn't PG. I was talking out of my ass to get through the interview but still praying to God that women out there would relate to my experience and be excited to buy book two. I had worked hard on it and really liked it, so I knew I wasn't selling crap. It was good stuff. After the entire seven-minute segment, I held up the book one last time and talked directly to Evan in the camera: "Hi, Evan, Mama loves you," I said.

With that, the red light on the camera went off, and I realized I had made it through my first interview. I had fifteen more hours of TV shows left that week, and then I could go home to my baby.

I walked off the stage, thanking my grandpa and telling him to stick with me for the next four days of press interviews. I'm happy to report he did. It was the end of the week, and I was completely successful at remembering all of my happy baby memories and making myself bury all of my pain and anguish while the whole country was watching.

COMING HOME was bittersweet. I badly wanted to run back to my baby, but facing the ugly road ahead made me want to take the long way home. I opened the door and ran to Evan and squeezed him so hard he squeaked like a toy. I could tell he was happy I was home, not by smiles and giggles, but by the amount of flapping going on. Only now I knew it wasn't a cute thing my Evan did, but a stim. Mommy was back and needed to figure out her next step.

As I lay in bed that night I felt so lost. At least when I was in New York, I could deny what was happening to make it through the press. I wished to God the doctor had handed me a pamphlet that said, "Hey, sorry about the autism, but here's a step-by-step list on what to do next." But doctors don't do that. They say "sorry" and move you along.

Chapter 10

ᕦ

Finding the Window

OH NO, the phone was ringing, and talking to anyone was the last thing on earth I felt like doing right now. Something inside told me to answer it, and since I'm good at listening to that inner voice, I did what I was told, and I'm damn glad I did. It was my sister telling me that she'd done makeup (my sister is a makeup artist) on a celeb who had an autistic child. She told me this mom would be calling me any second to talk and answer any questions I might have. I hung up and bit my nails off, waiting for her to call. Finally, a mother who could relate to my pain. Someone else who was in the public eye and could relate to faking happiness during rough times.

RING RING RING.

I dove for the phone. She told me about her son, and we compared stories on missing clues and so on. She then told me something for which I will forever be grateful. This next part of the conversation put me on my new life's mission. She said, "Jenny, there is a window with autism. And you need to pull him out of this window."

"What do you mean, a window?" I said.

"There is this window of time during which if you aggressively get him treatment, you can pull him out of autism." I immediately pictured myself pulling Evan out of an actual window, from that world he seemed so lost in and into my world.

"Is this true?" I said.

"Absolutely. But there are all sorts of things that must be done in order to get him there. My son is now in a normal school, but it started off a little rough. There is behavioral therapy that is proved to help these kids tremendously, and some moms talk about supplementation and diet."

"Supplementation? What do you mean by that?"

"Supplementing minerals and vitamins. You'll see, the more you get into it," she told me.

"Why didn't they tell me all this at the doctor's office?" I said.

"I don't know," she replied.

I thanked her immensely, and we said our goodbyes. I sat on my bed and stared at the wall in front of me. All I kept hearing in my head was "There is a window, there is a window, there is a window of time." What I needed to do was figure out how to pull him out. I stood up took a big deep breath, and got chills all over my body. If there was a 1 percent chance of saving my son, I was going to use all 100 percent of it. I had a mission. I was determined. No more "woe is me" shit. I leaped for my car keys and drove to the nearest bookstore. I ran up the stairs and desperately searched for the shelf on autism. I remember not being able to find it and was too scared to ask anyone for fear of being recognized. After twenty-five minutes of endless searching, I decided to tell my ego to shut the fuck up and ask for help. Within seconds, I was led to a shelf of books I never thought I would have to read. I grabbed ten of them and plopped down on the floor. As I read, I started to feel better. Not because I was reading warm and fuzzy stories about autism but because I was educating myself on every part of the diagnosis. I felt like I was going to take the driver's seat. What seemed like twenty minutes turned into three hours, and the bookstore was closing. I grabbed three books to take home with me and finished the first one in bed. I was really hoping to find one that said, "I cured autism," but I didn't. I remember thinking, "Well, maybe that's the one I'm supposed to write someday."

Before I shut off the lights, I went over some key points in the book. In it, a mom had talked about how she wouldn't give in to her child. If her child wanted a toy, she would make him try to say the name of the toy, even though she knew which toy he wanted. Now, let me explain something quickly. As mothers, we can read our children's minds so well that they can look at us and we know if they are thirsty, hungry, or tired, so we usually act without their having to say much. Even when they are infants, we are able to tell what all their different cries mean. This is where most mothers of autistic children get in trouble. We know our children so well that they don't even have to point or say that they want something; we automatically do it for them. This mother's book taught me to stop doing that and to make Evan try to say what he wanted with words and *then* reward him with the toy or the cookie, even if what he said sounded like "shjshuhdg."

I closed the book, walked into Evan's room, and stared at him sleeping. I leaned down to him and whispered, "I'm going to be really strong and do everything I learn from this point on to get you through that window, baby. I need you to be strong with me, Evan. This is gonna be a tough road for both of us, but I'm determined and promise to bring you back." With that, I checked his body for any fatal rashes and patted the top of his heart monitor as if to say "Good job keeping an eye on him." I kissed him on the head with the inner knowledge that I was on the right path. I had faith.

Chapter 11

$\backsim$

The Window Exists

THE NEXT MORNING I woke up and got Evan out of bed. He did what he usually did, which was run to the playroom and wait for me to open the door for him. I tiredly walked over in my big fat robe to open the door, but just before I did, I stopped. This was exactly what the book I'd just read was talking about. I knew exactly what Evan wanted, and I was going to give in to him without his saying anything. I got down on my knees and looked into his big blue eyes and said this word slowly to him: "OPEN."

He stared at me, not knowing what the hell this new game was that I was trying to pull off.

"OPEN," I said again.

He looked at the door and looked back at me and moaned.

"OPEN," I said again.

He looked at me, and this time started screaming at the top of his lungs.

"OPEN," I said again.

You would think a three-year-old would easily be able to say "open," but he couldn't. He could say "octagon" and "rectangle," which are objects, but not any verbs. "Why the hell is that?" I thought.

"O—P—E—N," I said again.

Evan looked at me and then started screaming loudly and kicking. I was amazed. He had never had a tantrum like this. I was pulling him out of his comfort zone, and he didn't like it. That was why he'd always been so passive—we'd kept his world just the way he liked it, and had done everything for him. Well, not anymore. I realized that the more he tantrumed, the more I was pulling him out of the window. This was only the beginning of tantrum hell.

"OPEN!" I said again.

More flailing and kicking and screaming. I knew this was going to take some time, so I plopped down next to the closed playroom door, determined not to give up. I had to see if what the book had said was right. If it was, I was going to put this kid through hell.

"OPEN," I said again.

More screaming and kicking. I watched my son's veins bulge from his head because he was so upset. I sat against that door and endured kicking, scratching, and loud screeches.

"OPEN," I said again and again, and after forty-five long

minutes, he stopped and looked at me. Then I heard, softly, "Ipin." I immediately threw open the playroom door and started screaming. My face was wet with tears of joy. "You did it, Evan! You did it, baby!"

It worked. It fucking worked! It didn't sound like "open," but to him, I know it did. He immediately saw the reward he got, which was me opening that door. I hugged him and praised him over and over so he knew that I hadn't been deliberately torturing him. I was still the mama who loved him dearly.

I was so excited about that working that I tortured the kid the rest of the day. I tried to get him to say almost every-thing that day before realizing that I needed to be happy with one success at a time. Don't overdo it. I felt a sense of promise and purpose; mostly, I felt hope that I could learn how to help my son. I just prayed to God to point me in the right direction. Fortunately, as you will see, He always did.

OUR NEW NEUROLOGIST, the protégée we had been re-ferred to, had called to check up on us. Judging only by my mommy radar, I really liked this neurologist. I let her know that there were no real side effects from the new white seizure meds. She said we were going to stop increasing the dosage for now and see what happened. I was so grateful we'd gotten to this point with no fatal rashes. I might have been overly cautious about it, but from what you've read thus far, wouldn't you be?

In the week after reading the books on autism, I still felt like I needed more. I sat down in front of the computer and Googled "autism." I was shocked by all the information and statistics I found. For starters, autism is way more common than I ever expected, and it keeps growing. It's the fastest-growing developmental disease, with a 10 to 17 percent annual growth rate. To break it down, every twenty minutes a child is diagnosed with autism. That works out to seventy-two kids diagnosed every day. Statistically, according to the Centers for Disease Control and Prevention, one out of every hundred and fifty kids is autistic, and one in every ninety-four boys has some form of autism. Of autistic kids, 1 percent to 10 percent are savants of some kind.

The other weird thing I saw was that Abraham Reichenberg, Ph.D., at the Mount Sinai School of Medicine, had discovered that men over forty were 5.75 times more likely to have a child with autism.

After all those statistics, I kept looking, and I found a site that said, "Autism is reversible."

I sat back in my chair for a moment and tried to decipher this. "Autism . . . is . . . reversible." That celeb mom I talked to had said that Evan could be pulled out of the window, and here I was seeing that this could be very real. The only reason I was still having an inkling of doubt was because no doctor had mentioned it to me. I'd gotten the "I'm sorry" and the nice shove out the door. Why in the hell isn't this on the fucking news every night if it's true? Why hadn't my trusted and famous pediatrician told me it was even a possibility? I felt so torn, wondering whom I could trust since my own doctors weren't telling me about hope. If you give me hope, I will take that road for as far as it goes.

I clicked on the link and began to read. As my eyes took in each word, I started to cry. The information wasn't what I'd thought it would be. I'd thought it would be about behavior tools, like I'd used with "open," but it wasn't. It was my first introduction to the effects of vaccines. I couldn't believe what I was seeing. My emotional guidance system was telling me I was on to something. Could this be the injury to the brain the doctors kept asking me about? I closed my eyes and had a flashback.

I was holding Evan at the pediatrician's office, and it was time to get his MMR shot. The doctor came into the room, and I said to him, "Evan's getting the MMR shot today?"

"Yep, it's that time," he said.

"Does he *have* to have it?" I said.

He stopped and looked at me and said, "Yes, he has to have it."

"Isn't this the autism shot or something like that?" I said.

"NO!" he yelled. "That's all bullshit. There is no correlation between shots and autism at all." Then the nurse handed me papers I had to sign before they gave him the MMR shot, stating that if anything happened to him from the shot, it was no one's fault. I looked at the papers and looked at John. "You're going to have to sign these, because I'm scared. I just have a weird feeling," I said. "Why would you have to sign papers to get a shot if nothing is supposedly going to happen?"

John glanced at the papers and signed them.

The doctor assured me yet again that everything was fine and not to worry. Those were just angry moms looking to point the finger because they had no one else to blame.

With that, I watched the nurse depress the plunger on the needle as John held Evan. I watched Evan scream, and that cry hurts me more now than it did that day.

As I sat back in my home office, I didn't know what to do with the information I was reading. Could it be real? Could all of this really be linked to vaccines? I figured in due time, little things would present themselves and lead me to the truth.

Chapter 12

ᘯ

Higher Calling

I ALWAYS KNEW Evan was in some way going to change the world. I had a very strong feeling about this one. I just didn't realize that it would have to be through me. It's funny how God works. Now I know why I became a writer in the first place. It was never to be the funny girl who wrote books on pregnancy and child-rearing. No.

Now I realized God had me write those books simply as a warm-up. To get moms' attention. This is the book I hope will shift the world. This is the book I was born to write.

I didn't want to leave my computer that night. I was so thirsty to drink up the knowledge that the Internet had to offer. John had come into the room but didn't seem interested in all the new things I was finding. I wished to God he would sit down next to me and say, "Hey, what have you found out?

Can I help you with any research?" Instead, we got into a fight. Every day we grew more and more apart, and it was breaking my heart.

BEEP BEEP BEEP BEEP!

Fuck! Evan's heart monitor was going off! I burst out of the office and was running like hell down that same hallway to get to Evan's room. I was screaming "No!" and felt my heart coming out of my chest. I couldn't take this anymore. I wouldn't take this anymore! I ran into the bedroom and leaped into his bed. He was not having a seizure, but his heart rate was way too high. I felt his body, and he was burning up. He had a fever, and I knew that heart rates speed up to fight off infection; that was what caused the alarm to go off. Sadly, I knew we weren't out of the woods yet. Having a fever induces seizures in kids who are prone to them.

I was at DEFCON one and took immediate precautions. I took Evan out of his bed and laid him in mine. I stripped him out of his clothes and immediately gave him Tylenol. I had to get that fever down. He was moaning in my arms, and I prayed to God he would not seize. I was just grateful I had the heart monitor to tip me off before anything happened.

I was asking John to get me cold rags, and *again* he started fighting with me. I think it was his way of freaking out and being scared, but my spirit was already so fried.

While holding my baby, I started crying and told John to leave me alone. I was so terrified of Evan seizing that my whole body started to shake. I was emotionally wrecked and kept thinking this was going to kill me. I kept praying to Mother Mary to help me.

I continued to give Evan cold juice and put cold rags on him. After pulling an all-nighter I knew we were seizure-free. My sisters came over the next day, and I remember the expression on their faces. I looked twenty years older, and every line on my face showed the sadness that was screaming from my soul. I still wouldn't leave Evan's side. They had to convince me to go take a shower, assuring me that they would lie next to Evan.

At last I listened to them and went into the bathroom to undress. I remember looking in the mirror at my new frail body, and I didn't recognize myself at all. My eyes looked so sad. Every part of me ached for someone to take away this pain. I knew no one could, so I opened my drawer and popped an Ativan and climbed into the shower. As I waited for the legal narcotics to give me a short break, I felt over-whelmed with loneliness. I yearned for some help. My sisters did their best, but they had jobs and their own lives and couldn't offer me the daily help I needed. I wished my mom could move out and help, but she still had her job back in Chicago. My father was also still living in Chicago but was blind in one eye, and I didn't want two special-needs people living in my home. (No offense, Dad.) I still didn't want my friends around; I couldn't stand their sympathy faces. I wished I had a husband who would have stood by my side.

As I let the water fall on my face, I wondered if I'd ever be able to go through this as a single parent. John and I were emotionally separated, so realistically, I guess I already was.

Chapter 13

 exo

The Show Must Go On

I GOT A CALL the next week to say that my second book, *Baby Laughs,* was number seven on the *New York Times* best-seller list. My agent said, "Aren't you excited?"

I tried to muster up the best acting I could and squeezed out a "yes." But all I really cared about was that I would be able to get another book deal and be paid to stay home and take care of my baby.

"I've got an idea for another book," I said.

"Oh yeah? What's that? 'Toddler Laughs'?" she said with excitement.

I had always planned for the next one to be "Toddler Laughs." My heart broke with the knowledge that my toddler was different from most. I had no idea what it was like to raise a normal toddler. "Toddler Laughs" would never exist. I held back a tear and replied, "No, 'Marriage Laughs.'

There are so many funny things that happen in marriage. I think I could do a great job with it."

"All right, I'll go shop it!" she said.

I hung up and sat back in wonderment. How the hell was I going to write another comedic book about marriage and motherhood when my marriage was falling apart and my son was autistic? Looking back, I'm amazed at the strength it took for me to put one foot in front of the other, but I did. Day after day. Instead of getting mad at God, like I'm sure a lot of people do, I decided to make Him my buddy in this. I remember saying to Him around this time, "God, I know you gave me an autistic son for a reason. I know I'm supposed to do something with this, and I don't quite know what it is yet, but I need you to help me out. I need to be always pointed in the right direction. I need the messages to be loud and clear so that I can serve my purpose in your calling."

When you make God your buddy, He answers fast. Within a week my mother-in-law called me with a lead. She said she had done some fund-raising once for a doctor who headed up an autism program at UCLA. I jumped on the lead and made an appointment. They said to me on the phone that they were going to do "a full comprehensive assessment in all areas of development" so they could determine what services Evan needed. I was scared. I didn't want to hear any more about how behind he was in areas of development. I didn't know if I could possibly take one more piece of bad news.

The day came for Evan to be evaluated, and I put him in

his best outfit. I always thought if he looked adorable, people would see past any of the "flaws" that would be flapping around. John and I took Evan inside, and they put us in a room separate from Evan. You would think a stranger taking your son out of his mother's arms would cause a three-year-old to say, "No, I want my mommy," but he didn't. He didn't even notice that I was gone. John and I watched Evan through a one-way mirror and were frustrated because we couldn't hear anything. We didn't know if he was responding to the simple tasks they were asking him to do. After thirty minutes, they invited us back in the room for another forty-five minutes of testing.

"Evan, can you point to your feet?" the female psychologist said. Evan looked off into space.

The woman got within a few inches of his face. "Evan, can you point to your feet?"

Evan looked at her as if she were speaking Spanish. I blurted out, "He knows that they are feet. He has said 'foot' to me before, while touching his foot. I don't know why he is not responding." My voice was quivering. "Try his nose. He has pointed to a picture and said 'nose' before."

The woman looked at me and then at Evan. "Evan, can you touch your nose?"

Evan stared at her again as if Spanish were coming out of her.

"Evan, can you touch your nose?"

He sat there. I became so frustrated that I leaned in and took Evan's little hand and pointed it to his nose and said, "Nose! Remember, Evan? You've said 'nose' before." I looked to the therapist and said defensively, "I think you have him on an off day, because I know he knows where his toes and nose are."

The therapist said, "You're right, he probably does know where they are, but he doesn't understand the question."

"What do you mean, he doesn't understand the question?" I said.

"It's called auditory processing. Evan isn't able to process the entire question. He might comprehend some of the words in the sentence, such as 'nose' and 'toes,' but he isn't sure what he's supposed to do with that information. For example, he might have stored only the word 'nose' or 'toes,' but not 'touch.' Therefore, he doesn't realize that I want him to touch those items."

"So you're saying he doesn't understand what I'm saying?" I asked.

"No, I'm sure he understands some words, but he can't take in that much language. Let me continue." She asked, "Evan, what does a cow say?"

Evan stared at her blankly. A three-year-old should be able to answer such simple questions. I was starting to crumble inside. I'd had no idea that my boy didn't have a clue what I was saying.

"Evan, what does a cow say?" I jumped in, hoping he would answer me.

Then John jumped in. "Evan, what does a cow say?"

Evan stared at us blankly.

"This is crazy!" I said. "He has a cow stuffed animal and holds it up and says 'moo moo' all the time."

"He might very well know the cow says 'moo.' However, when asked the question 'What does the cow say?' he simply doesn't understand he's being asked a question and is supposed to provide an answer. Questions with more than one or two words are too much for him to retain and process all at once."

I held back my tears but was crying inside. We had a long road ahead of us. At three years old, my son couldn't understand a basic question that a one-year-old could answer. I was scared. I was very scared. I was hoping he would excel in some upcoming tasks, but I didn't want to get my hopes up.

Next they pulled out the tiniest blocks for him to pick up and build a wall. He had trouble using his pincher grip to grab them, and instead of making a wall, he struggled to make a tower.

"This is very common with autism. Fine motor skills are somewhat weak," the therapist said. I sat there and tried to absorb more painful words to describe things wrong with my son.

"Does he walk on his toes?" she asked.

"Yes."

"Does he look at things or toys out of the corner of his eye?"

"Yes."

"Does he have any stims?"

"Yes, he flaps."

"Does he ignore you when you call his name?"

"Yes, well, sometimes."

"Does he stare at fans or spinning objects?"

"Yes."

"Does he play with door hinges, objects like that, instead of toys?"

"Yes"

"Is he affectionate, and does he show warmth and love?"

I was about to answer, and stopped. Time stood still at that moment. I wanted to reply, "Yes, all the time, he hugs me like all little boys hug their mommies and gives me kisses." But he didn't. I honestly had never noticed that I wasn't getting the physical love that most mommies get. I really didn't need it, because love is energy, and I felt it. His love was *louder than words*, and our connection was very deep. If Evan never spoke a word, I would be able to read his mind and feel a love connection that could be felt by the whole universe. I answered, "Does he show love? He *is* love. And I feel it every day."

The therapist looked confused about which box to check and went on to the next test.

After an agonizing hour, the therapist smiled and said they would mail us a report. She directed me to a building across the street to check out the UCLA Early Childhood Partial Hospitalization Program, a program for autistic kids. I said goodbye and struggled to cross the street. I looked at John, and he looked as bad as I felt. We had taken a serious pounding that most parents never have to endure. I know parents who can't listen to their child's preschool teacher saying their kid wasn't paying attention today. Can you imagine hearing that your three-year-old has the comprehension of a one-year-old?

We walked into a building and went up to the seventh floor. We had met with the program director, who showed us the class that was currently in session. There were only five children in the class, and I was amazed to see five teachers. The director said it was a very intense program, and because it was located in the hospital, it would be ideal for Evan, with his seizures.

This seemed like a really good place. I could tell these people knew exactly what they were doing. I asked when Evan could start, and the answer almost made my heart shatter: "The waiting list is about a year."

"A year?" I thought. "But there is this window of time to fix him. That window is partially closed in a year." I asked with desperation, "How could this be?" The director told me that funding was limited, and there were many more children than there were teachers available.

She then said, "Have you started with the Regional Center yet?"

"What's that?"

"How come you don't know about the Regional Center?"

"Well, no one told me. I never got the sorry-your-kid-has-autism-here's-what-to-do-next pamphlet."

She was so sweet, guiding me to the next thing I needed to do. She handed me a phone number to call the local district and register Evan. The Regional Center was where children with special needs got services provided by the state.

I filled out the application for the UCLA program, and the director said it was possible to jump the list if a kid was a match.

"What do you mean, a match?"

She said, "We like to pair the children with other children who might be at the same 'level,' to encourage socialization. So if there is a child coming in our class soon who matches Evan's evaluation, we will give you a call."

Because I'm a firm believer in hope, I put it in God's hands and prayed for the best.

Chapter 14

∽

The Wait Continues

AS WE DROVE HOME, the car was silent. John and I were still fighting, and I had just found out that my son had pretty much no idea what I was saying. During this ride, I wondered how other mothers with autistic kids dealt with it. Were they also lost in knowing how to get help? I couldn't believe the red tape and the maze with no directions. What if I hadn't started searching for help? What if no one ever told me there was help? Would I be sitting at home, watching my son play with door hinges until he was sixteen? I prayed for all the mothers like me across the country that God would give them a message through someone or something. I knew someday I would be a messenger, but in the meantime, I prayed every autistic child was getting the help he or she deserved.

When I got home, I called the Regional Center. They

said I had to call a different number and set up an appointment. But before I could do that, I would have to wait for a letter stating that Evan was registered.

"How long does that take?" I asked.

A few weeks, the woman said. After I got the letter, I would have to take a parent course, but there was no room available for two months, and after that, Evan could get evaluated, which would take some time, and then we would see if he was qualified to get funding for services.

"Okay, hold on, lady," I said. "So I'm looking at about six to eight months of paperwork and bullshit before I can get funding to help my baby?"

"Yes."

"But if autism can be helped dramatically in a certain amount of time, why do you guys make the wait so long when we could be curing our kids in that time?"

"There are just way too many children with autism, and we don't have enough funding to pay people to process all the applications," she said. She gave me a number to an agency that would eventually come to my house to do therapy, once it was funded. She told me to call and put Evan on the list.

Jesus Christ, ANOTHER LIST! I hung up and called a company called CIBA, California Institute of Behavior Analysis, considered one of the best, and Evan deserved nothing less than that.

I said, "Hi there, I would like to put my son on the waiting list for behavior therapy."

The woman said, "Okay, the waiting list is a year and possibly longer."

"You've got to be kidding me!" I said. I couldn't believe this. It felt exactly like someone saying, "You have cancer, and we have chemo for it, but we're not going to give it to you until a year from now. Good luck!"

I put Evan on the list and prayed to God yet again, because that was all I could count on at this point.

I hung up the phone and walked into the playroom to see what Evan was doing. As usual, he was spinning an object. I got down on the floor and looked at him and said, "Hey, little bird, you know what a cow says, don't you?" He ignored me and kept spinning the toy. So I picked up the toy and put it away and sat down in front of him again.

"What does a cow say?" I said. He looked up at me and stared so hard into my eyes that I felt it deep in my soul. I could see so clearly in those big blue eyes that he wanted to tell me, but he couldn't find the answer in his head. I was about to start crying, so I handed him his spinning toy and continued my tears as I began to do the laundry. Forty-five minutes had gone by, and I was about to unload the dishwasher when I felt this tug on my leg. I looked down and saw Evan blinking his big blue eyes up at me. He said, "Moo."

I stood there for a moment in shock, then: "Oh my God! Yes, Evan. MOO! MOOO!"

I picked him up and started screaming and laughing and giggling and twirled him all around the living room. He said

"MOO!" He had figured it out. It was bittersweet, because it had taken him forty-five minutes to find the answer, but I was still so happy and proud that he had searched this whole time so he could come up to me and say my favorite new word in the English language: MOO!

I knew the months ahead would seem like years while I waited for services, so I decided to educate myself on diet intervention. I ordered a book called *Special Diets for Special Kids Two*. In the past year, even before all this seizure stuff came about, I'd noticed that Evan had started to look weaker. He had become paler and developed blue rings under his eyes. His balance was horrible. I never knew what to make of it, and his "good old" pediatrician never seemed worried. But I began to worry.

I pulled out some photos from the year before of Evan sitting on Santa Claus's lap and looking malnourished. I couldn't understand why. He ate; I gave him Flintstones vitamins. He also couldn't tan. I know that sounds weird, but living in California and being a blond kid, he should have had some color, but he never did. Just pasty. I wondered if there really could be a correlation between his nutritional health and autism. Why was this talk about diet and nutrition considered controversial and talked about only by other moms?

As I waited for the books about diet to arrive in the mail, I was planning what to do for Evan's upcoming birthday. It made me depressed to think about healthy children running around and laughing when I knew Evan would be off spinning in circles and flapping his hands in a corner. I still wanted to keep everyone away, so I canceled his party and had my sisters come over to sing with him.

DING-DONG.

"Oh no, visitors!" I thought. "Don't they know I want to hide in my cage with my boy and not let anyone in? How dare they come without calling?" I opened the door, and standing in front of me were two boys wearing white shirts and ties. It was the Mormons.

"Hello, how are you doing today?" they asked.

"Oh, hey, guys, listen, I'm really not in the mood right now. I would rather have you come back when I feel more on the upswing again."

"Maybe we can help you with that upswing," they said in chipper voices of hope. Okay, let's observe this moment for a second. I have two young Mormons at my door, asking me if they can help get my upswing back. I so wanted to say something dirty, but considering I'd talked about the poor kid's balls last time, I decided against it.

"Sorry, boys, not right now, okay?"

"When should we come back?"

You have to give them credit—they are very determined to talk about their faith.

"Um, when my kid starts getting better, then maybe I can give you an honest ear. Right now I just can't."

"Okay, thank you, and have a wonderful day."

Thanks, Mormons, you, too. I closed the door and prayed my faith would stay as strong as theirs.

Chapter 15

∽

I LAY IN BED, staring at the new fifty-inch flat-screen TV that I had pushed up against my bed. It was my new baby monitor. We had a spy camera hooked up in Evan's room that attached to this giant monitor. The monitor was half the size of the bed, but I didn't care. I needed one that big because every hour throughout the night, I would open my eyes and stare at the screen to watch Evan inhale and exhale. Even though he was connected to the heart monitor, I felt like I still needed to be the backup system ensuring his safety. John had started to get angry at me because all my attention was always on the baby monitor, and he felt ignored, invisible. If I'd had it my way, I would have been living in Evan's room. I rolled over, as usual, with my back facing John, and I prayed to God he wouldn't ask to have sex. Sadly, sex was torture for me during this phase of my life. The only fantasies I wanted to imagine were Evan being able to say, "I love you, Mommy." I had no desire whatsoever to get off and honestly didn't care if I never had sex again.

Finally

THE BOOK came in the mail. *Special Diets for Special Kids Two*. I couldn't wait to read it and fill my eager heart with more knowledge. I was blown away when I read that mothers often noticed that their autistic children were malnourished because they couldn't absorb nutrients from food. After beginning a gluten- and casein-free diet (wheat- and dairy-free) with vitamin supplements, mothers reported huge changes in their children, sometimes even recovery from autism. I had to make sure I wasn't hallucinating, so I read that again. Could it really be true? Could diet make that much of an impact? And why would wheat or dairy affect the brain? And if this was true, why wasn't it on the Channel 7 news at night? Why wasn't it on *20/20*? Why did moms have to find out on their own?

I asked Evan's pediatrician about it, and he said it was horse shit. "Another desperate attempt at healing autism," he said. I didn't know what to believe. All I knew—and I'm going to say it again—was if there was hope in anything, I was going to give it a try. Although I vowed not to make Evan a guinea pig in testing every new thing on the market.

What I got from the book was:

Evan was possibly born with a weaker immune system;

getting vaccinated wreaked havoc in his body, and mercury caused damage to the gut (the gut being the home base for your immune system), which caused his inability to process certain proteins, and one could see the result of this damage when he consumed wheat or dairy. It messed with his little body so much that he wouldn't respond when his name was called, he behaved like a drunk, and the list goes on. Through removing wheat and dairy, this book proposed, some of these behaviors could dissipate or disappear.

I found it completely fascinating and exciting that a diet could help. Like I said before, I couldn't believe that the gut could correlate to the brain and that what I fed Evan could have a direct link to his behaviors. But I was inspired and willing to give a diet a shot. I couldn't sit on my ass doing nothing while waiting for services, so I made this my new mission.

The book said to start off slow, maybe remove dairy first and then wheat the next week. I wanted to see results fast and decided to cut him off cold turkey. Not a good idea, but it was interesting to see him go through withdrawal, almost like an alcoholic. That was my first tip that the book could be right. He tantrumed and gnawed on the back of his fist. There were times I wanted to throw in the towel, because listening to tantrums all day long would make any mother reach for the vodka. I didn't, of course, but I'll tell you what I did instead. I bought an iPod. This helped more than you can imagine, and I recommend it to many mothers with autistic children. Sometimes our kids tantrum *all day long*, so the only quick relief is to throw on that iPod while you're making dinner in the kitchen and listen to the sounds of Enya to take you away.

After a couple of weeks, the tantrums had diminished by half. I continued to research online all the different gluten- and casein-free recipes and started to find things getting easier. Thank God for Google. You can find anything on that search engine. I ordered all sorts of noodles and cookies that Evan was "allowed" to eat.

The Window Opens a Little

ABOUT THREE WEEKS had gone by with Evan on the diet, and I was putting away dishes in the kitchen when I felt a tug on my leg. I looked down and saw Evan's big blue eyes staring at me. It wasn't his normal glazed-over look. He seemed clear-eyed. He tugged on my leg again, and I got down on my knees and said, "Hey, little bird, what's going on?"

He looked at me again and said with all of his might, "Want . . . to . . . go . . . swimming."

John was standing next to me at the time and leaped into the air. "Did you just hear that?" he screamed.

My eyes filled with tears, and I nodded. I couldn't believe it. Evan had said a sentence. This was huge. HUGE! It was everything. The window had just gotten wider, and I was pulling my baby out! John picked him up and ran outside, and they both jumped into the pool with their clothes on.

Chills went through my whole body, and I cried as John and Evan splashed in the water. Up to this point Evan would say only one word at a time, and only words for objects. The fact that he had just blurted out a four-word sentence was honestly a miracle. I knew it was the diet that had helped clear the fog, because within that week Evan responded to my calling his name every time I said it. He also didn't seem drunk. Mind you, he was in no way cured from autism, but just three weeks prior, he had been locked in a world of spinning toys and ignoring people. Now he was actually trying to tell me what he wanted and was responding to people in the room.

Even though this progress made me so happy, I couldn't help but be pissed off that doctors weren't telling moms to at least try it. They really were against the diet. My thinking is that if the diet works on *some* autistic kids, that would link it to vaccines, and God forbid that happened. Doctors will never admit it, and it's a useless war to try and fight.

Evan still suffered from multiple environment and food allergies. After educating myself on the diet stuff, I believed that all of his allergies had something to do with autism and not just bad luck. I had no way of proving this yet, but all the puzzle pieces were starting to fit together. I knew I still had a mountain to climb, but at least the first little hill had been a victory. I was even more eager to keep going.

Chapter 16

∽

RING RING.

I got a phone call from my agent, asking if I wanted to do a show for E! called *Party @ the Palms*. It was in no way a dream job, but it had two key factors that made me say yes. One was a paycheck; the family was desperate for some income. The second was they would shoot most of the show in three days and require me to go to Vegas only once a month for those three days. That allowed me to spend most of my time with Evan and still bring home the bacon. Before I left for my first taping, I taught John exactly what Evan's diet required and how strict it was. I went over the white seizure meds and explained what dosage we were up to. I told him to be alert for fatal rashes; even though we had made it to a safe dosage, I still worried. I tried to jam all the info into John's brain the best I could. I flew to Vegas, hoping the three days would go by in record speed and that Evan would be as safe as I had left him.

While in Vegas working my butt off, I realized something valuable: how good it felt to escape the world of autism. Even though I was working, not resting, it felt so good to be doing something for me. I had forgotten how important it is to have your own work, your own time and sense of accomplishment, that is just yours. When you are the mother of a sick child, you're going to put yourself on the bottom of the priority list. This job made me realize how much I missed myself and how I needed to bring some balance back into my life. When a mom is healthy and happy, her kid will benefit. I flew back feeling refreshed, even though I had worked thirteen-hour days.

When I walked in the door, I hugged Evan and kissed him till he was pink with kiss marks. I noticed he was a little off and wondered what was wrong. He seemed dazed, and when I asked John about it, he responded with "I don't know." I looked on the counter and saw a milk shake, half gone. I figured that John had given him dairy. I picked up Evan and brought him into his playroom and turned on *Baby Einstein*. I didn't want Evan to ever be in the room when his parents fought, so this is what I tried to do before an argument. And let me tell ya, there was one coming. I walked back into the kitchen, looked at John, and said, "I want you to move out." He responded, "What's the big deal if he has wheat or dairy once in a while?"

I couldn't figure out why he would go ahead and give to Evan what I had worked so hard to get out of his body. The only logical explanation I could muster up was that he thought Evan was breaking through on his own and that the diet had nothing to do with it. The only good thing that came out of this incident was that we both saw the result of what the dairy did. I continued to tell John I wanted him to move out, but he didn't. I finally asked him to get into marriage counseling with me, and he agreed.

I didn't know what to expect from marriage counseling. We sat there and explained our stories and talked about the relationship in general, and then we topped it off with an autism dressing. The therapist told us that when most couples come into counseling, it's already too late. I was afraid she was right. We agreed to see her twice a week in the hope that doing aggressive therapy might speed up the healing of wounds. Only time would tell how well it was working. In the meantime, I continued my efforts to save Evan.

My Mommy and Me friends were still reaching out to me, and I still didn't want much to do with them. I was very depressed about my failing marriage and Evan's autism, and I did not need to be reminded how well their children were doing. It's sad to say, but when I went to parks with Evan, I would watch children his age talking and playing with their moms, and I hated them for their happiness and the wonderful simplicity of their lives. I can admit that I looked at young kids with evil eyes because I was in so much pain. With every word, they reminded me of how behind Evan was. This was another reason we stayed far away from playdates. Just talking to my friends on the phone and hearing their kids interrupting felt like knives in my chest.

This is why a huge majority of mothers of autistic children no longer have friends with "normal" kids. It hurts too much. There is also a natural tendency to brag about your kid or tell a funny story, and that was the last thing I wanted to hear. I just hoped in due time Evan would be well enough to play with his old group of friends, or that I would eventually come to grips with being around healthy children. But for now it was too hard.

Chapter 17

∾

Help Has Arrived! Thank You, God.

I RECEIVED A PHONE CALL from the UCLA ECPH autism program, telling me that Evan could begin soon. He matched another child's level, which would help both children in their socialization therapy. A few months had passed since Evan's evaluation, and I was hoping the therapists at UCLA would see a difference in him since we'd started the diet. I hung up the phone and did a happy dance, celebrating that the recovery train was moving ahead.

I bought Evan a new set of cool clothes and a cool lunch box. He had never gone to school more than three days, and even though it wasn't really school, I pretended it was, just for my own ego. We pulled in to the parking lot and walked along the sidewalk to head into UCLA. Along the way, we had to pass three different buildings with sliding glass doors. Evan flipped out and screamed and yelled until I brought him to each sliding glass door to watch it open and close, open and close, open and close. Sadly, for the next three months, this was the obsessive-compulsive routine we had to do every morning. If we missed or cheated past one sliding glass door, Evan turned into Satan baby. Therapists would say not to give in, but I didn't have the energy to wrestle a strong three-year-old into a building every day. So every morning I allotted time to watch sliding glass doors open and close, open and close, open and close.

On the very first day, just before we walked into the building, I stopped in my tracks to stare at the sign above the door. Tears came to my eyes as I read it quietly to myself: NEUROPSYCHIATRIC HOSPITAL. It's impossible not to be heartbroken when you're bringing your child to a place where they keep mentally ill people. There were no paintings of animals or cartoon characters on the wall, like at a preschool. Instead, I saw only people who apparently had brain problems being wheeled in and wheeled out. I closed my eyes and envisioned coming back to visit this building when Evan was sixteen, and talking about his recovery. I continue to hold that vision today whenever I face any pain on our recovery road.

After the twelfth opening and closing of the doors, we made it inside. We walked to the elevators and waited for more doors to open. Two employees passed Evan and me, and I heard one say to the other, "Dude, that's Jenny McCarthy. What's she doing in a neuropsychiatric hospital?"

His friend responded with "Kinda fitting, don't ya think?" They both laughed and continued down the hall. I knew I couldn't come into the building every day wearing a beard and a mustache. I had to face the fact that I was likely to be recognized on a daily basis.

The doors opened, and we got on the elevator. There was a sweet older couple on there already. They took one look at Evan and started talking to him. "Hey, little boy, what's your name?" Evan just flapped and flapped and flapped his arms. He was so distracted by the moving elevator that any human noise was drowned out. To him, the sounds of the elevator shaft were beautiful music.

"His name is Evan," I said.

"Oh, Evan, you're such a handsome boy. Are you a fan of Superman?" the little old lady asked him. It was so hard when people would come up and talk to Evan; I knew that my kid had no idea what they were saying unless it was in a *Blue's Clues* episode. I did all of his answering for him before anyone could catch on. Like many mothers of autistic children, I'm sure, I have responded with "Oh, he's just being shy today" to get out of the uncomfortable zone. The elevator door chimed open, and Evan and I escaped before another question could be asked.

As I walked down the hallway, I felt good about Evan being in this program. I felt lucky. To explain it as simply as I can, the program offers something called applied behavior analysis (ABA) therapy. ABA is a proven treatment that works on the causes and reasons for undesirable behavior and then teaches positive alternatives. On staff were a speech therapist, an occupational therapist, a recreational therapist, a social worker, and my favorite, a nurse. I knew I would get to know her really well. Someone else I could trust to look out for fatal rashes!

We opened the door to the classroom, where Evan was greeted with love and affection. I sat with him for a bit and carefully watched the other children in the room to see where they were in comparison to Evan. In the other baby books I have written, I talk about comparison shopping: all of us mommies out there who see other babies in parks or stores and eye them up and down, comparing milestones, looks, and behavior. I was still doing that, but on a much harder level.

The program director had me kiss Evan goodbye and told me that I could watch him for the next hour through a one-way mirror. I immediately bolted into the observation room. As I closed the door behind me, I saw two mommies who had jumped up to greet me. I could tell by their looks that they had recognized me. I saw excitement and some relief in their smiles, to know that celebrities also could have kids with autism. After saying some quick hellos, they immediately started firing out questions.

"Do you know about the diet? The gluten- and casein-free diet?" one mother said.

"Yes, I figured it out. Evan has been on it for a few months now," I said.

"Do you know about chelation?"

"Chelation? No, what's that?"

"It's to detox mercury out of the body. You know about the mercury, right?" she said.

"Yeah, to some extent. I do believe that's how damage was done to Evan's immune system."

"Well, you have to get it out. You have to chelate the mercury out."

"How do you do that?"

"You need a DAN! doctor."

"A what?"

"A DAN! doctor. It stands for Defeat Autism Now! These are the only doctors who can help you with detox and supplementation."

"I don't understand the supplements part. I read a little bit about it in *Special Diets for Special Kids*."

"Supplementation is huge. Most of our kids have a leaky gut that's caused by an overload of candida, or yeast. The best kind of multivitamin to start out with is Super Nu-Thera, from Kirkman Laboratories."

Then they started to hand me phone numbers of doctors and Web site info. I felt so overwhelmed and, at the same time, relieved that I had just met women with whom I could share my pain and recovery stories.

It was time to move out of the observation room. The two moms brought me downstairs to a private lounge where parents wait while their children are getting therapy. Most mothers in the program stayed the whole six-hour day, and I planned on hanging right there with them. I had no choice. I wanted to be as close as possible to Evan at all times, and I needed to start writing my new book. How I was going to write a comedic book on marriage from a neuropsychiatric unit where my autistic kid was getting services and while my marriage was falling apart was beyond me. But I knew something that ironic and weird could only happen to Jenny McCarthy.

TICK-TOCK-TICK-TOCK.

Finally, it was time to go get Evan. I ran upstairs with all the other mommies. We piled into another observation room. It was in this room that I realized I would someday be a voice for mothers of autistic children. There were about ten of us smashed into this tiny observation room where we got to spy on our kids for the last fifteen minutes of class, and it made me cry. No, it made my heart shatter into a billion pieces yet again. As we watched our kids on the other side of the glass trying to speak, I started to look over the other moms' faces. None of them knew I was watching them; their emotions were written all over their faces. We all were suffering so badly. We all were watching our kids struggle to do basic stuff, and it was killing us.

One mom had her hands pressed up against the glass, whispering, "Say it, Mikey, say the word."

Mikey was a cute, chubby seven-year-old who still hadn't spoken more than a couple of words. He had the sweetest demeanor and looked so eager to try and speak one word. He just couldn't get it out. Unfortunately, this is all too common—as many as four in ten autistic children may not speak at all.

One little girl had a machine she used to speak with, and

another little boy just enjoyed bouncing his butt on a ball while humming. It was great to watch the kids improve because of the program, but it was also heartbreaking to see the kids who didn't progress at all. One thing that all these kids had in common was their love of music. The sound of singing brought smiles to the faces of children who you never thought could have that kind of response. I looked back over at all the moms squeezed inside the observation room with me, and I said, "Ya know, there's a special place in heaven for mothers of autistic children." They all looked at me with an inquisitive smile. "And the first round of shots is on me." They all laughed. It was great to see smiles come on their faces. I needed to lighten up the heaviness of reality behind that glass, for their sake—and mine.

The door that separated the two rooms finally opened, and I ran to Evan. I picked him up and twirled him around. I kissed him so hard and so much that he squirmed away from me in pain. I didn't care. I was then approached by the speech therapist, who said to me, "Is this evaluation correct?" She held up Evan's first evaluation from a few months earlier.

I said, "Yes, it's correct, but since then I started him on the diet, and he has broken through some, don't you think?"

She smiled and said, "Yes, I do. It says here that he couldn't point to his feet or nose during that evaluation, and he did both without a problem today. That's a pretty great improvement." Victory! Proof I was on the right path. Someone else had seen it, too, and it kept me motivated to keep trucking along.

The gluten- and casein-free diet was working. I could tell Evan felt really good on it. He was so much more present. I knew it was crucial to keep going with it, because it would allow him to absorb all the speech and behavioral therapies.

I left the neuropsychiatry hospital that day with a good feeling in my soul. I had met some great women, Evan had responded well to the therapies, and I had gotten to see a fascinating display of sliding glass doors.

Chapter 18

&

Autism Moments

I WAS FASCINATED that the children in Evan's class had such similar behaviors. I had thought most of the characteristics—arm flapping, playing with toys incorrectly, loving toys with gears or anything that spun—were just Evan's, but they weren't. They were autism characteristics. To give you an idea of what I mean, I would point to a door and say, "What's this? This is a . . . What is this, Evan?"

Instead of saying "door," he would respond with "Rectangle." Or I would point to a stop sign and say, "What's this?" and he would respond with "Octagon."

I couldn't say no to either of those, because technically, he was right. He just had trouble seeing past shapes. Now I knew why, when I would take him to the zoo, I could say, "Look at the monkey" that was right in front of him, but all he saw and wanted to look at was the monkey's cage. He was so enraptured by the cage design that we left the zoo without his noticing one freaking animal. This was back in my denial days, when I thought he was destined to become a mechanic. I also found it fascinating that he could recite an entire *Blue's Clues* episode yet could not say a complete sentence of his own.

Sometimes you can't help but lose your patience. Every mom can lose her temper when her kid starts to aggravate her, but if you have an autistic kid, sometimes you need the patience of a saint not to jump off a roof when you're listening to the repetition. Like if I asked Evan, "Do you want noodles for lunch?" he would either respond with "noodles" or recite a sentence from *Blue's Clues* over and over: "It's a fun bag surprise, it's a fun bag surprise, it's a fun bag surprise, it's a fun bag surprise, it's a fun bag surprise, it's a fun bag surprise, it's a fun bag surprise, it's a fun bag surprise, it's a fun bag surprise."

This would not stop until I repeated the exact sentence back to him. I would have to say, "It's a fun bag surprise," and then he would stop. If I responded with, "Yeah, Evan, I heard you," he would keep saying, "It's a fun bag surprise" until I said it, too.

I had never noticed how Evan didn't give me much affection because, like I said before, I *felt* loved. But as he got older, I started to crave my little boy holding his arms up to me and saying, "Mama, hold me." When I would try and put him on my lap and hug him while watching a movie, he would sort of push me away. (Kind of like we women do when we are PMSing and our husband tries to give us a hug and we respond with a shove and "Not right now.") My heart ached at this point for a snuggle and some affection. I was so drained and exhausted from all that I was doing that I prayed to God someday my boy would want to hug his mommy so much, I would have bruises.

Chapter 19

෴

OPEN CLOSE OPEN CLOSE OPEN CLOSE.

Yes, Evan and I were once again watching the sliding glass doors on the way to autism school. It was a beautiful morning, and I felt grateful that God had led me to another place that would help Evan heal. After we made it to the classroom, I kissed him goodbye and slid into the observation room to eavesdrop. The speech therapist had taken Evan and seated him across from her. I watched her pull out a toy sheep. She said, "Evan, is this a dog?" He responded, "Dog." He always repeated the last thing you'd said. He knew it was a sheep but didn't understand the question and had just heard "dog," so he repeated it. She then prompted him, "Nooo, it's a shhh . . . " Evan said, "Shhheeep."

As I sat there watching my boy understand words, I recognized for the first time that he had never said "no" or "yes" to me. He would repeat back. Example: "Evan, do you want juice?" He would say, "Juice." A tear came to my eye as I realized that he didn't even understand the meaning of "yes" or "no." At three years old, he should have known something as simple as that. I left the observation room brokenhearted.

I stood in the hallway, wondering what to do with myself. I knew I would be coming here every day for the next few months, and I had to decide where I would wait out the six hours. I had my laptop with me because I had to start writing my next book. Setting up shop in the Burger King across the street did not feel right to me. Then again, neither did writing in a neuropsychiatric hospital. I headed down to the room where the other autism mommies had brought me the previous day. This was where they all hung out, but I was worried I would get caught up in conversation instead of writing.

I opened the door and was greeted by a group of moms who had already heard my child was in the program. Before I could even say "hi," they greeted me and started telling me yet again about diet, detox, and how I needed to be the one to spread the word about autism being an epidemic. I told them probably in due time, but I just wanted to fix my boy right now. They were all very sweet and incredibly knowledgeable about autism, and I took in as much as I could.

This mom named Lisa had begun telling me a little bit of her story. Her son, Jake, started off like every other normal baby, happy and saying the usual couple of words. After she took Jake to get his MMR shot, she noticed that he had runny black stools for months afterward. This was followed by his no longer being able to fall asleep, and he started to become withdrawn. She brought him to his doctor, who said, "He's fine, don't worry. He's just a little behind; get him a speech therapist." So she did, and he started to learn some skills. It was then time to give Jake his hepatitis C vaccine. She didn't think twice about the vaccines having any correlation to what was happening to Jake, so she went ahead with it. She said after that shot, everything went to shit. He lost all skills and completely lost the ability to answer "no" like he used to. He then was diagnosed with autism. By age three, he began forty hours a week of therapy followed by any other treatment Lisa and her husband could find. They sold their house, got a new one, refinanced it, and borrowed money— all to pay for autism expenses that insurance does not cover. She lost her best friend after her friend asked if Jake was contagious. Jake was seven years old when he began the UCLA program and functioned at a two-year-old level. Jake is now nine years old, and Lisa is still working her ass off with him. The latest treatment they're trying is hyperbaric chamber treatments. She said she would forever work on fixing Jake and would stop at nothing to make him better.

Listening to her determination and strong will made me smile at her and say, "I think we're going to become the best of friends." Any woman willing to go the distance like I am will be a good friend of mine. I'm proud to say Lisa has become one of my best friends.

Other moms in the school talked about how they didn't think autism was caused by vaccines. They said their children's showed symptoms of autism from a very early age, almost birth. Why some autistic children start off normal and then regress, while other autistic children don't, still leaves me baffled. I read an article about genetics research that said autism is much like cancer, in that it takes so many forms, and that's why so little is known.

I told the other mothers I was grateful for all the information, but I had to write an entire book by the time Evan was done with the program, so I was going to throw myself in the corner and dive right in. They were excited for me to be writing my third book and completely amazed that I could think of anything humorous to write about in the midst of all this upset. As I turned on my computer, I looked back at them and said, "Ya know, I've always been able to find humor in things that seem painful, but how I'm going to find humor in my marriage right now is beyond me."

It was going to be one hell of a task. I typed the heading on the first chapter—"Bribing for Blow Jobs"—and stared at the blinking cursor. Now what? The room fell silent as all the mommies waited for me to start typing something. To contemplate writing funny things about my husband, whom I not only didn't get along with but who was also never around, was killing me. I sat there for a moment longer and turned back toward them. I said, "Is anyone else having marriage problems?"

Every hand in the room flew up. And it wasn't just that room; as I said earlier, the divorce rate in families with autistic kids is very high. A woman named Mary said, "Honey, you thought your husband did nothing to help out before? Now throw autism in the family, and you have a husband who is no longer around." I looked at all the other mothers' eyes, and I saw so much pain. My eyes filled with tears. I knew they were the only ones trying to save their kids. They went on to talk about how, if the moms didn't exist, our children would not get better. Our husbands would not research endlessly for answers or talk with other parents to look for tips they may have missed, and they would not do all the tedious shopping and cooking to ensure that their kid followed a strict diet. They would do what they do, which is stay as busy as possible and have someone else deal with it. I'm not husband bashing right now. I'm honestly stating what all the other moms seem to be in total agreement about: Our husbands disappear when we need them the most.

In my Google research, I even found a couple of psychological studies that noted this difference. Moms and dads process autism differently. While dads note that having an autistic child has caused severe difficulties for their families, they don't feel that it has a significant personal impact on them. This is not true for moms. Moms take it personally, and maybe that's why they do the work.

I looked at these amazing women and asked, "Why aren't you guys all divorced, then?"

They answered, "Because we moms had to quit our jobs to bring our children to therapies. We can't afford to be on our own."

I said, "Okay, how many moms here would get a divorce if you had plenty of money to live on your own and had proper help for your autistic child?" *All* of them raised their hands, and a chill went up my spine. This is not how it should be. We're already suffering so much, watching our children struggle; to see other women suffering because their husbands don't help pains me even more. They all stared at me, and I stared back at them in silence. I think they, too, were amazed by our mutual feelings.

That Led Me to Marriage Counseling

AS I SAT THERE next to John, staring at the marriage therapist, I burst into tears. My face turned eight shades of red as I cried for Evan, for me, and for my so badly wanting my marriage to work. Everything seemed broken, and I wanted things fixed. I still wasn't sure I could go through this journey on my own; I was really trying in therapy to get to the bottom of what was wrong. But I was beginning to realize that autism wasn't breaking up the marriage. The marriage had had a big crack in it before autism came into the picture. The therapist said when a crisis like this happens, it brings to the surface the existing problems and fast-forwards the inevitable. All the bullshit that lies around in a marriage is brought to the table all at once. She was right, because on my table was a feast of problems. Still, I was going to give it a try. We left with "tools" that would supposedly help when dealing with arguments.

I remember driving back in the car with John, thinking, "This sucks." I was going to give us another shot and hoped to God that John would also try.

Chapter 20

∽

RING RING.

"Time to go back to work," my agent yelled. You have to do your next episodes of *Party @ the Palms* in Vegas, and you leave in a couple of days." I hung up with a sick feeling in my belly because Evan had caught a bad flu. He had been sick on a weekly basis since starting school. They say that this is normal when kids get thrown into classes where everyone spreads germs. I agree with that, but Evan was sick on a whole other level. He'd had a fever for about three days, and the fever was getting very high at moments. Because Evan was prone to seizures, I had to rotate Tylenol and Motrin every three hours without missing a beat.

I was supposed to be getting on a plane to Vegas and leave my sick boy behind with his father and part-time nanny. I had a bad feeling about this and decided to use my entire paycheck for this episode on a private plane to fly in and out. I wanted to come home that night and be with

Evan; the next day I would fly back on Southwest Airlines. That night I came in the door and crawled into Evan's bed and woke up every three hours to give him Tylenol or Motrin. The next morning I had to say a painful goodbye to my sick boy and fly back to Vegas. As soon as I landed, I walked right in front of the camera and started working.

Less than five minutes into working, my heart started beating unusually fast. I began to feel dizzy and became very nauseated. I had never felt anything like this before. It didn't feel like a flu. I couldn't explain what was happening, but I could no longer stand up right. This was all captured on camera. I slumped to the ground and started shaking. I looked up at my sister Joanne, who was with me, and said, "Something is wrong with Evan. I know it. I feel it."

She handed me her phone, and I dialed frantically. As the phone rang and rang, I kept feeling sicker. John finally answered, but before he said anything, I said to him, "Evan's having a seizure, isn't he?"

John responded, "Yes, the paramedics are on their way." I dropped the phone and ran outside to the car and headed to the private airport. I was numb. I couldn't believe my boy was seizing again. I couldn't believe I was physically feeling what he was feeling. I'd heard about moms knowing something is wrong with their children when they are far away from them, but I had never felt it before. It was and is very real. I prayed to God this seizure would not be as bad, considering he was on anti-seizure medication, but all I could do was pray. I ran inside the private airport and started screaming, "Does anyone have a plane I could take to Los Angeles?

My son is being rushed to the hospital. Please! Please! Somebody help me!"

People don't usually run into private airports screaming this sort of thing, but I didn't give a shit. I ran up to a lady behind a desk and threw my credit card at her and said, "Please find me a plane to get home. PLEASE." She jumped on the phone and started making calls. I stood at the window, watching plane after plane take off, and held myself back from running onto the runway, begging for a ride. I closed my eyes and tried to stay connected to how Evan was doing. I couldn't tell anymore. I just held on to visions of him being okay.

"I found you a plane!" the woman at the desk shouted. I ran over to her, and she told me it would be about an hour for the pilots to show up. It would cost seven thousand dollars. I told her I didn't care how much it cost, I just needed her to tell the pilots there was no need for a shower and a shave. I just needed them to get here faster! She said she would do her best. I paced and paced until one hour went by and my pilots arrived. We all ran to the plane together, and they started the engine. It was music to my ears. I was going home to my boy. My sister Joanne flew back with me, but we didn't say a word to each other. I think we were both praying too hard. It didn't matter, though. I was relieved to have one of my wingmen with me.

Looking out the window of the plane, I watched the sun setting in the desert. It was so incredibly beautiful that I knew God was with me. I was trying to make sense of everything, my purpose in this, and what *I should do next*. I asked

God if this was a sign of something I was missing. I just didn't know. I surrendered all worries and daydreamed of Evan as a teenager. I always found this soothing in crisis and also considered it a positive visualization. I saw him bringing home his first girlfriend; I saw him at a meet, winning a race; and I saw him in a tux going to the prom. I looked back out the window and saw that we were about to land. Thank God, I was home.

When I made it to Evan, he was alert and talking. This time his seizure lasted only two minutes, compared to the twenty minutes they used to last. I was relieved to hear that. My heart was broken, though, because I hadn't been there for him at such a scary time. I asked the nanny what had happened, and she told me that John didn't think Evan needed the next dose of Tylenol yet, so she didn't give it to him. I almost fell off my chair. So what had happened was that Evan's fever had spiked too fast, and he'd seized. I couldn't get angry—if I dwelled on the past, I couldn't focus on the present, and the present was where I needed to be. I plopped down in bed next to Evan and held him tight in my arms. I whispered in his ear, "Sorry that happened, little bird, I promise I'm gonna try and make sure it never happens again."

Chapter 21

∽

Keeping the Faith

IN THE COMING WEEKS, Evan kept getting sick. Sicker than usual. I couldn't relax, because I kept worrying he was going to have a seizure, and I was going to make *damn* sure it wouldn't happen on my watch. Night after night I kept watching his heart monitor and praying not to hear it go off. I was in a constant state of panic.

Why was he getting sick so often? *Why* couldn't he fight off little bugs?

Back at UCLA

I DECIDED TO OBSERVE Evan in speech again. I watched behind the one-way mirror as the speech therapist held up a dog toy and said, "Evan, is this a cow?" I found myself shaking my head, as if he could see me through the glass, as if I were helping him cheat during a test. I so badly wanted him to say no. He responded with "Cow." My heart sank as I prayed for "yes" or "no" to come out of that cute little face. The therapist then prompted a "no": She made a brilliant move and took out some chips: Evan's favorite, Fritos (completely gluten-free and legal on my strict list of snacks). I saw his eyes light up as she held up a chip. She said, "Evan, do you want a chip?" He looked at her and then at the chip. The therapist repeated, "Evan, do you want a chip?" His little mouth said, "Chip!" She asked again, "Evan, do you want a chip?" He looked at the chip and said, "Yes." I leaped into the air! I know the therapist must have heard me, because the walls were shaking with me dancing around like a crazy person in the observation room. He'd said "yes," and he'd understood it. That day will stay with me as much as "moo."

I walked downstairs to the mommy waiting room with the biggest smile on my face. "This school rocks!" I thought. Who cared if it was inside a neuropsychiatric hospital. They were making that window wider, and I would forever be in debt for their determination.

I briefly told the other mommies about the "yes" moment and sat down to try and write some more pages in my book. I was really struggling. All the mommies were talking again, and all I wanted to do was be with them and share stories. So I closed my computer and plopped down next to them. This Tuesday's conversation was about how it had been too difficult to keep their kids' old playdate friends since the diagnosis. Almost all the mommies had pushed their old friends away when their child could no longer play with the rest of the bunch. Like I described earlier, I could completely relate. I told them I was going through the same thing, but I at least held on to the friendship with the moms even though my heart couldn't bear to have Evan involved in any playdates at this time.

Another mommy walked into the room. I had not met her yet, but from their excited hellos, it was clear that everyone else knew her. I quickly learned why she was so welcomed. She was the Yoda of moms with autistic children. She knew freaking everything. I began to question her about her findings, since she was so in tune with the latest treatments. She talked about B12 shots, which were shown to boost speaking because they had something to do with neurotransmitters; she also talked about hyperbaric chamber treatments, and intravenous immunoglobin (IVIG) treatments, which helped children's immune systems. My ears perked up at this. I said, "Evan gets fevers almost weekly, and I don't know what to do about them."

She told me to go to a DAN! doctor and at least get started with B12 and have further testing from there. I begged her to call her doctor for me and see if she could get me in, since all the moms had already told me that DAN! doctors have a one- or two-month waiting list. She picked up the phone and said she would give it a try. I heard her tell the office that it was an emergency. Then she gleefully told me I was in. Thank God!

As we continued to talk about alternative treatments for our children, I noticed the room separating into two sides. We were no longer talking as a whole anymore. There was a group of moms who didn't want anything to do with what we were talking about. They slumped into a corner and had a "woe is me" attitude. I decided to eavesdrop on both conversations.

The "woe is me" moms were talking about how they didn't get to shop or go to the beach with their friends anymore, and the "I'll try anything if it will help my kid recover" moms were trading success stories about the latest treatments. I couldn't understand why *all* the mommies would not be up for something that *could possibly* help their kid. I thought it might be because they didn't believe in alternative treatments or because they didn't want to hope—thinking that if a treatment didn't work, that might destroy them even more. My other theory was that they enjoyed the victim role. I know that might sound mean, but I'm sure you've met people who are constantly having shit go wrong in their life. They complain and play the "don't you feel sorry for me?" game. I've met so many moms like this. I wonder if their belief that nothing is working for their child is exactly why nothing is working.

Then there are the moms who have tried everything under the sun to help their kid, and though nothing has worked, their faith in or acceptance of the situation has led them to still be able to stay positive. They have every right to play the "woe is me" game, but they don't. They take comfort in knowing that they at least have done everything they could for their child.

I left UCLA that day with more skip in my step. I believed with all of my heart that I was going to pull Evan out of the window, and I continued on my path to do just that.

A few weeks after meeting with our first DAN! doctor, I was amazed by all the supplements and treatments they throw at you after the first test results come in. Many people say that there are a lot of doctors taking advantage of hopeful moms by having them do too many treatments on their kid. I tend to agree, which was why I made up my own rules. This doctor wanted me to immediately start chelation (excreting mercury), whereas I felt it was important to get Evan's immune system functioning before I did something so harsh to his body. I planned to introduce one new treatment at a time and to test only things that I felt were safe and logical.

I did start Evan on B12 shots twice a week, and I was honestly blown away by what I saw. His speech doubled on the days I gave him the shots. Even his teachers at school were amazed by the sudden boost in his speech. The window was opening a bit more.

What was not improving were his constant fevers. He also was becoming more and more allergic to things, and it was driving me crazy. He became allergic to even more foods, the rugs in the house, his pillow. You name a possible allergen, and this kid was sensitive to it, with hiving and itching. I felt like I was the lead detective in a mystery novel, trying to put clues together as to why Evan was having certain symptoms. I refused to ever put a Band-Aid on the problem. If I was going to fix Evan, I had to find the culprit for the sudden allergies and consistent fevers. I dug in and continued to do more mommy research. I've always hated unanswered questions, and you can be damn sure I was going to get to the bottom of everything that came my way.

Chapter 22

RING RING RING.

Oh no! It was my agent again. I had to go to work. I was so grateful for the money since autism costs a *fortune*, but I wanted to stay on this path of healing Evan. I finally agreed to work on a movie in Canada for a week, because it would be money in our account, and it would force me to sit in my hotel room and finish my book. I was three fourths done and really wanted to get to the finish line. I taught John exactly what was needed to care for Evan and hoped the nanny would do most of it. Then I packed a bag and flew to Canada.

After a long day of shooting, I plopped down on my bed and opened my computer. I began typing the chapter about anniversaries and how sweet it is to remember all the wonderful moments in your marriage, and I burst into tears. I realized I was completely lying throughout the book about my supposedly wonderful marriage. I couldn't do it any longer.

For a girl like me, who tells the whole ugly truth about everything, holding back the truth was tearing me apart. I shut my computer and cried like a baby. After an hour or so, I stood up, looked out the window, and came to the realization that I officially wanted a divorce. I called up my book agent and said, "Guess what? I'm rewriting my book and changing the name from 'Marriage Laughs' to 'Life Laughs.' Trust me on this one." I then called home for the eight hundredth time that week to see how my boy was doing. I spoke to the nanny for my check-ups. I didn't feel like fighting with John. My heart wasn't there anymore.

Soon enough, the week in Canada was over, and I was flying back. As we were approaching Los Angeles, I started to get a nervous belly. I was already feeling scared about finally telling John I wanted a divorce, but this was a different kind of nervousness. I couldn't shake it. I was flying with my manager and told him something was bothering me. He said I probably just missed Evan. But as I walked through the airport to get into the car, I started having that dizzy, shaky feeling I had experienced before when Evan was having a seizure. As the feeling became stronger, I started to cry. I knew Evan was seizing again. I jumped into the car and called John's phone. He answered by saying, "Evan is having a seizure, and we are pulling up to the emergency room at UCLA." I knew it. I felt it. I wasn't there for him again. But what was I going to do? Bills had to be paid. This was tearing me apart. It was torture. Since we had started treatment, Evan had never had a seizure on my watch, and it killed me that he kept having them when I was gone.

I arrived at the emergency room and ran to find Evan. His little body was in a postictal state—basically, he was unconscious. Evan's neurologist, the protégée we had been referred to, came in and talked to us about increasing his dose of the white seizure medication, and I agreed. I stared at my little bird in a hospital bed yet again, and I wondered how we were going to survive all these setbacks and fear and disappointment. Autism is hard enough, but when you throw seizures into the mix, you can only imagine the beating my heart took.

In the midst of all this, I still had the will to change the way things were. So even though my heart and soul were suffering, I continued to stay positive about our future. I envisioned Evan being healthy and happy. We were released from the hospital later that day.

New Beginnings

A WEEK LATER, I was in the car with John and was staring at him during a red light. He looked at me and said, "What's going on?"

I stared at him for a beat and replied, "I want a divorce."

He pulled over to the side of the road and stopped the car. "So that's it? You're not even going to try?

"We did try. It's not working. Are you happy?"

"No," he replied.

"Well, neither am I."

We sat there in silence, and even though I was relieved

that I had made this decision, I grieved the loss of the marriage. Like most people, I had believed that I'd married for life and was so sad that the relationship had failed. I was sad for John, and for Evan and me, and for our little family.

We went home and tried to figure out who got what. Because this was California, John had the right to take half the house and half of all monies and half of my paychecks for the next three years. I was the breadwinner, and that was the law. I wish there were a part of the law that excepted mothers of autistic children, but there wasn't. I settled with John by giving him pretty much all the money in the bank account. I was starting at zero, but at least I got to keep my home. I decided to refinance the house to cover the costs of my upcoming autism bills and move on. Again.

As John packed up his last box of belongings, I looked at Evan, who was watching his dad pack. It was the only moment I was actually grateful for autism, because it made it impossible for Evan to emotionally connect with what was going on. Even when John said, "Daddy's moving into a different house," Evan stared off as if his father were speaking a different language. Right before John was about to leave with his final box, the doorbell rang. As I walked to the door, I was cursing my friends whom I thought were coming to visit. Didn't they know I didn't want to see anyone? And this was an especially awkward moment.

I opened the door, and standing there were the Mormons again. OH MY GOD. I looked at them and said, "You guys have some seriously bad timing."

"We only need a moment of your time," they said with innocent pleading eyes.

I said, "Listen, I really do appreciate you both coming here and doing a healing on my son a while back, but it continues to not be a good time for me to hear about your religion. I promise you that I will let you in and let you talk your butts off once I can get a grip on my life."

Before they could even say, "We could help you get a grip on your life," I smiled and closed the door.

I turned around to find John kissing Evan. I knew this was hard on him, too. He looked at me and said goodbye and walked out the door. I watched him walk down my driveway. Never in my life did I imagine asking my husband and Mormons to leave my house on the same day.

But as they all walked down my driveway together, I felt a sense of peace come over me. New beginnings. I had become a much stronger person since the diagnosis. I had realized that I deserved happiness and my son deserved perfect health. I wasn't the type of person to wallow very long, and I had a goal that I was determined to meet. The clock was ticking, and if my plan was to pull Evan through that window, I had to look forward.

Chapter 23

~

Open Close Open Close Open Close

EVAN'S PROGRESS at the UCLA autism program was nothing short of miraculous. He was up to six-word sentences, had mastered "yes" and "no," and showed interest in peers. Other parents were amazed by Evan's development. At times I felt bad, because even though they were also doing the diet and supplements, some children weren't responding as well as their parents had hoped. This is where I learned about the wide range of differences in autistic children. Though some were much more affected than others, I still had hope and prayed every day for all of them.

The week before Evan was going to complete this program, he became sick again. My nerves were so fried from being on seizure alert that I was starting to turn gray. I started opening my mouth and asking everyone I knew in the autism community for help, and thank the sweet Lord I got the answer I was looking for. One of the best DAN! doctors in the country was seeing a child whose mother ran an autism charity. I begged her for help and she made a phone call for me.

Luckily, the best DAN! doctor in the world was not in Timbuktu. He was in Texas. His name was Dr. Jerry Kartzinel, and on the first visit, he had Evan tested for everything and saw numerous deficiencies. But the one that was causing Evan's consistent ailments was his weak immune system. Dr. Kartzinel told me it was imperative to send Evan to the best immune doctor in the world, down in San Diego, for further testing. I couldn't understand how Evan's immune system was so damaged. Dr. Kartzinel simply replied, "Vaccines."

I still wanted to learn the specifics of how vaccines damaged the immune system, but I knew I couldn't sit down and do adequate mommy research on all of it quite yet. It was driving me mad, though, to learn that so many ailments, especially of the gut, were linked to autism. I'd always thought autism was just a brain disease. Some neurologists still think so, but if they would visit all of the autistic children, as I now know, they would see bloated "Buddha" bellies, severe constipation, and other gut issues. Evan had been on laxatives and consistent enemas for years because he had trouble with his bowels: another bonus that many mothers of autistic children endure.

Home Bittersweet Home

EVAN WAS NO longer in the UCLA program. I had hoped the state would have the paperwork done to fund Evan's in-home therapy, but no such luck. The decision I had to face was, did I just sit around and wait for funding—which could still take months—or did I self-fund, because treatment was imperative right now in order to pull him through the window. I called some agencies that did in-home therapy and asked them how much it would cost me to self-fund. Most of them replied with, "Seventy-five dollars an hour, and Evan was approved for thirty hours, so that would be twenty-two hundred and fifty dollars a week." My voice cracked as I said, "Holy shit," and I sank into my chair. I had taken out a pretty large second loan on my house, so I knew I could cover it for now. I replied, "Okay, let's get started," and hung up the phone. I was nervous, considering I was also paying the world's best speech therapist $150 three times a week; a physical therapist $120 a week; a music therapist $60 a week; and a play therapist $300 a week. Throw a nanny into the mix, and I was having to pay $4,000 a week. When I talked to other families about how they dealt with so many expenses, the story was always the same: They'd refinanced their house or borrowed money from family members.

On a bigger picture, there was a study in 2006 that showed the economic costs associated with autism were $35 billion a year. Treatment for a preschool child with autism typically cost over $50,000 a year. The *New York Times* has estimated that only 10 percent of afflicted children are getting those services, and as a nation, we're letting down twenty-five thousand more children every year.

Autism is not getting the financial support it needs. In 2005 the National Institutes of Health dedicated only 0.3 percent of its budget to autism. Though on December 7 the Senate authorized $1 billion for autism research, autism is still very far behind in private funding. Leukemia affects one in every twenty-five thousand and has $310 million in private funding. Pediatric AIDS affects one in eight thousand and has $394 million in private funding. Autism affects one in hundred and fifty and has only $15 million in private funding.

I had faith that money would continue to come into my life as quickly as it was going. Just know that if I ever come out with my own dumb perfume line, this is why.

DING-DONG.

"Please don't let it be the Mormons," I thought. I opened the door to see Evan's first in-home therapist. It's very odd to have someone come into your house every day and walk around with your child. Being a mini-celebrity, I thought, "I hope they don't tell people that I have dirty socks lying around my house." They're really not interested in my socks, thank God. Evan was beginning in-home ABA therapy. It was the same therapy that UCLA did with him, and judging from his improvements there, I gotta tell ya, this shit really works.

One of the difficult things was hearing my child scream,

sometimes for three hours straight, from the other room. An example of a lesson that would cause him to blow would be the therapist trying to make him say "I want" instead of "Evan wants." Evan always referred to himself as "Evan" instead of "I," so this was an important thing to work on, but Evan didn't think so. I so badly wanted to say to the therapist, "Couldn't you just do *fun* things with him so he doesn't scream?" But that would defeat the purpose of therapy.

That's where a lot of moms get into trouble. Autistic kids want to stay in their comfort zone, zoning out on spinning objects. Pulling a child out of this window of autism is a bumpy ride, and I was prepared for Evan to be sore by the time I was done with him.

One of the most wonderful things Evan learned before he left the UCLA program was the concept of First and Then. It might not seem like a big deal to anyone reading this who does not have an autistic child, but these kids don't understand the concept of waiting. Food in a restaurant needs to come immediately. Waiting does not make sense, and they will tantrum like a crazy person until they get what they're waiting for. I remember people staring at me while Evan tantrumed in the grocery store line. People would stare at me like "Wow, she totally has no control over her kid. She needs to get a grip over her child and teach him to be patient." Some people have actually said those words to me, and in response, I've shouted in their face, "He's autistic, you asshole."

Once Evan mastered "FIRST put toy in box, THEN I'll give you cookie," it changed everything. I was able to teach him things this way, and he improved so much faster because of it.

I was so grateful that I was able to pay attention to what Evan's therapists were doing with him. If you really want to see that window open, pay attention to what they're doing, and mimic it when they leave. Without a doubt, I was Evan's number one therapist, and I know someday he'll be forever grateful.

Chapter 24

༄

Waiting for My Angel

AS TIME MOVED ON, I lay in bed every night wondering what my future would look like. I had always envisioned Evan healthy and happy, but what did Jenny look like? How did I envision myself? One night I leaned over and grabbed my Archangel Oracle tarot cards and shuffled them and pulled out a card. It was the same card I had picked over and over again the past few months. It was starting to drive me crazy. It said that I was to help teach the Indigo and Crystal children. I remember thinking, "Is there some sort of a tribe in a different country, and I'm supposed to go and help these Indigo and Crystal children?" As usual, I put that one to the side and kept shuffling. I then said, "Tell me what I should be focusing on for my future." A card jumped out of the deck and I turned it over. I always loved when they leaped out of the deck—I felt like it was a shout-out from my angels. The card said, "We are working on your soul mate relationship."

It had been a few months since John had left the house, and even though I was relieved not to have all the fighting and tension in the house, I also felt hungry for some companionship. I had been lonely in the marriage for a very long time, so I was craving love and affection from a loving guy. I would lie in bed night after night praying to the archangel Michael to help me cross paths with a man who was the closest replica to a living angel to walk the earth. Not too much to ask, right?

I wanted someone who had pure love to give and a heart open enough to receive. I closed my eyes night after night and envisioned meeting him. I finally began to sleep peacefully.

ESCALATOR ESCALATOR ESCALATOR ESCALATOR ESCALATOR ESCALATOR.

"Hi, Megan. Hi, Steve. Oh, hey, Sarah."

That was me, now knowing all the names of the people who worked in the stores next to the escalator in the mall. Evan and I continued our almost daily ritual of riding the escalators. This became a reward for him for either going pee-pee in the potty or simply saying a whole six-word sentence on his own. I surrendered to being a mommy who didn't have a child in the kiddie section of the mall. I found joy in watching my little boy experience ecstasy while watching the escalators go up and down. It was during this time when I stopped being angry at little kids who would come up to me and start talking about *Bob* the freaking *Builder*, even when I knew Evan couldn't understand *Bob the Builder*.

I started to feel a shift in me. I was accepting what *was* and not hating the world for what should have been. I came to my own conclusion—that acceptance does *not* mean giving up. Nothing was going to stop me from pulling Evan out of this window. I just simply loved him and was proud of who he was no matter what. I found myself loving his flapping, his tiptoe walking, his love of fans, door hinges, and escalators. I thought, "So what. If he grows out of it someday, great; if not, he comes here after the prom with his girlfriend and they ride escalators till the sun comes up. Evan *is* perfect."

Once I'd brought joy and acceptance back into my heart, I felt like enjoying a night out on the town with my sisters. I got dolled up and was looking forward to having a cocktail and not mentioning the word "autism" for a whole two hours. I kissed Evan good night and had the nanny sit next to him, watching the beeping of the heart machine.

My sisters and I went to a Hollywood party that was filled with celebs trying to look cool, including me. I hadn't been out on the town in a long time and wasn't even quite sure what clothes were in fashion. I was looking around the room, enjoying my cocktail, thinking how weird it was to be single again. I had no intention of ever getting married again and wasn't sure about a relationship, because Evan's needs were so demanding. I wanted to enjoy my time with my sisters without feeling like I had to meet someone.

As fate would have it, I was moving across the room when someone stopped me to introduce me to someone. I turned around and was introduced to this really cute guy. I smiled and shook his hand and began some small talk. It was so nice to talk to someone at this point who had no idea about the history of the events that had happened in the past year. Chitchat flirting continued a few more minutes, and I figured I'd better get back to my sisters before I made an ass of myself. I said, "See ya later," then went back to boogie on down with Joanne and Amy.

As the night progressed, there was a little voice in my head that would not shut up. It was an instinct or a feeling that I had not felt in a long, long time. There was something so incredibly beautiful in this guy's energy that I couldn't keep myself from glancing over at him. I kept thinking, "Jesus Christ, Jenny, get a grip." But I couldn't help it. He was glowing from across the room as if God was putting a flashlight over his head so I could see him through the crowd. I pulled my attention back to my sisters and danced with them and continued to have fun on my night out.

About an hour later, I sat down to take a break and felt someone plop down next to me. It was that same guy. I smiled at him like a total dork, and we shared some more small talk. I didn't know how he was going to behave, but he turned out to be this calm, sweet guy who had so much warmth that I completely enjoyed sitting and talking with him. He was surprised that I wasn't the outrageous wild chick who beat up boys on MTV. The night ended, and I gave him my number and went home with my sisters. It was a great night, and even if all that ever happened was a great conversation with a really sweet guy, I felt lucky.

Chapter 25

༄

Back to School

I DECIDED to try and have Evan start preschool again with "typical" children. "Typical children" is how the autism community describes children who don't have autism. A shadow, meaning a therapist, was required to go with him; otherwise, Evan might not be able to understand what his peers were trying to say to him. He would also need help with whatever the teachers asked the kids to do, like putting away toys and then sitting in a circle. Evan would maybe understand "put toy in box" but then would get stuck standing at the toy box and need help getting to the circle.

About a week after he started his new school, he began to get sick again. If a classmate got sick, Evan would always be the first to catch the bug. And then Evan's cold or flu would last for two weeks instead of the usual few days. By this point, he had been on so many antibiotics that I was afraid they were going to stop working on him. As soon as he was feeling better, I would put him back in school so he could actually learn how to be social with other children, and he would immediately get sick again. I was doing my usual routine of lying in bed with Evan and putting cold cloths on his head to keep his fevers down when I received a call from the cute guy at the party. All I could think of was how incredibly awful I looked and how, if he knew the road I had been on, he might find himself really busy all of a sudden. He asked me to come over and watch a movie, and I said yes. I told him it couldn't be until a week from now because my boy had the flu and I first needed to make sure he was healthy. He understood, and our first date was set for the next weekend.

Evan did get well enough for Mommy to have her second night out in a very long time. I went over to the guy's house with the hope of simply having some really nice small talk and maybe a killer make-out session. It turned out to be exactly that. We talked, watched a movie, made out a little, and I headed back home to be with my boy. It was really nice during this time to have someone about whom I could daydream while doing mundane therapies with Evan. I had no expectations of where the relationship could go or what was happening between us. I was just enjoying being a girl on a cute boy's sofa who looked pretty in her new blouse and wanted to feel liked by him.

As the weeks continued, I was seeing him only one night of every weekend. Evan was starting to act a little more kooky during this time, so I had to make sure my focus remained on opening the window and not on getting lucky. Evan's behavior had started to concern me. He had developed a bad obsessive-compulsive disorder that experts say happens with a lot of autistic children. But I wasn't buying the fact that it had developed on its own, and so intensely. One day out of the blue, with no warning, Evan wouldn't stop screaming until all the doors in the house were closed; none of them could be even slightly ajar. Also, if you washed his hands and there was a drop of water still left on them, he would go ape shit. Then he started to itch his ears all night long while he slept, and he flopped around as if he were humping the bed. It was very weird to watch a three-year-old hump his bed in his sleep. I couldn't understand why Evan was suddenly so obsessive-compulsive in his behavior and demands, and why he seemed to get worse every week. My motherly instinct told me that something was wrong, that I was missing a sign. And I was determined to figure it out for Evan.

Chapter 26

∾

Crazy Evan

EVERY MORNING I would wake up and walk into Evan's bedroom, and he would be angry and psychotic toward me. I started to become scared of my own child. I would get him juice in the morning, and he would scream and say, "Other cup," so I would put his juice into a different cup, and then he would scream and cry and say, "No, other cup." So I would get the other cup. Mind you, this is *not* something you should ever do, because it's giving in to autistic behavior, but when it happens every day and you cannot listen to the screaming anymore, you give in to your child's demands. So morning after morning, I was pouring his juice into other cups until we got right back to the same freaking cup we'd started with. I would put his food on the table and plop him into the chair, and if the chair was two degrees over to the left, he went crazy and would not stop screaming, sometimes for hours. All I kept thinking was how absolutely unacceptable it was for me to believe that this new severe OCD was now just part of his autism. I knew there had to be a health-related issue that went with it.

Day after day, it was getting worse. I started not to recognize this crazy child. The therapists were clearly handling him better than I was: When they walked in the door, Evan knew they weren't going to let him get away with anything.

Even my sisters were freaked out by the new manic Evan. What had happened? What the hell had happened? I started crying every night, wondering how much crap this child had to endure. I was so confused and upset and didn't know whom to turn to. He started banging his head on the floor, sometimes for hours. I couldn't watch it anymore. I needed help. I had to stop everything in my life at this moment and get my boy back to where he was just a few months ago. I begged God to give me the autism I had back then, not to leave me with whatever was happening to my boy.

I called my agents and told them I would be taking some time off. I had to figure this out before Evan started putting his head through the glass windows. I felt relieved, knowing I was taking a break from work, because, until I could get Evan healthy again, I couldn't play mom *and* actress. Sadly, I also knew I couldn't play girlfriend. I was planning on traveling to Mars and Jupiter to save Evan, so for now being a girlfriend was not written in the stars.

I went over to the cute boy's house and cried all over his shirt. I told him that I couldn't be with him at this time in my life but hoped someday in the future we would cross paths again. It was so hard to do, but when your child is sick, everything else becomes secondary. I still hoped and prayed that one day I would sit next to him on the sofa, watching movies and kissing. That was the thought I held on to as I drove away.

Chapter 27

୶

Finding Answers

THE ONLY MEN in my life now were Evan, Dr. Texas and Dr. San Diego. Dr. Texas is Dr. Kartzinel, the DAN! doctor, and Dr. San Diego, I will call him, is the world's best immune system doctor. Dr. Kartzinel told me that Evan's stool had a lot of yeast in it and that I should have started him on antifungal medication a long time ago. He felt that many of Evan's OCD behaviors were side effects of severe candida overgrowth, which wasn't uncommon in an autistic child. He explained that when a person takes antibiotics regularly, the intestines get stripped down, and then yeast or candida overgrowth occurs, causing OCD-like and erratic behavior. He started Evan on Diflucan, an antifungal medication. He then had us go down to San Diego for more intensive immune system testing.

When I met Dr. San Diego, he told me that IVIG treatments could help restore Evan's immune system. Basically, that consisted of taking other people's blood cells and putting them into Evan's body through an IV every month, for six months. Before that could happen, we had to test Evan's immune system to see if he was even healthy enough to handle the treatment. The tricky part of this therapy is that your immune system has to be somewhat active, in case your body needs to fight off an illness from the donated blood.

The results came back, and I couldn't believe what Dr. San Diego was telling me. He said that Evan was not eligible for this treatment because his immune system was that of a dying AIDS patient. I didn't know what to say. What the hell had happened to this kid's immune system? How could he score not just low but the absolute worst? Dr. San Diego told me I needed to keep Evan out of school and away from public germ areas. I said, "How is he ever supposed to learn to be social with peers if I can't send him to school? Can I send him maybe once a month?"

The doctor looked at me with stern eyes and said, "No, not until his immune system gets built back up."

I said, "Well, how do I help him do that?"

He said, "Time, maybe. Sometimes it doesn't come back very much at all."

I sure as hell wasn't going to listen to that. I wanted to know how this had happened. What is the correlation between a weakened immune system and autism? I was going to make sure Evan's immune system got better. It was time to dig and get my doctorate from the University of Google.

In the meantime, I had started Evan on the Diflucan. Not only did this entail giving him prescription meds; worst of all, I had to limit his diet even more. I was already denying him wheat and dairy, but now I had to make sure he avoided all sugars, including fruit, and anything else that yeast loved to grow on.

I couldn't believe the things that took place shortly after his first week's dose. He went full-blown Exorcist on me. If his head had been able to turn in a 360-degree circle, it would have. His eyes were bulging with rage, and he was grinding his teeth so much when he slept that I thought he would have none left in the morning. He also threw up, and his pee was cloudy and painful to the point where he would scream when he peed. Each poopy diaper was loaded with yeast.

I couldn't believe what I was witnessing. My sister Joanne had visited a lot during this severe die-off period and also couldn't believe what she was witnessing. I had sympathy for Evan's pain, but after starting my heavy research online, I knew that this extreme reaction meant I was absolutely on the right track.

Chapter 28

∽

The Sun Was Peeking Through the Window

TWO WEEKS into this yeast madness, it was as if the clouds moved away enough for a little sun to shine through. I was lying on the bed, watching a cartoon with Evan, when all of a sudden the most amazing thing happened. Evan giggled at a joke on the TV. My whole body went into shock. Had Evan just laughed at a joke? Then it happened again. I slowly looked over at him and saw a smile on his face. He'd really gotten the joke! My son had gotten the joke! Do you have any idea what that meant? Probably not, if you don't know that much about autism, but trust me, it's HUGE!

My eyes filled with tears, and I stood up on the bed and started screaming at the top of my lungs. It was such an abstract joke that I knew his being able to understand and get the joke meant he could be breaking through. This was much bigger than his being able to say a six-word sentence. Much bigger. It meant he was understanding subtext and emotion. It meant he was understanding language in a more complex way. It meant he was no longer in a confused daze but was growing mentally and emotionally. It meant sunny skies where before there were only clouds.

I continued to scream and jump on the bed as Evan stared at his crazy mom in awe. I'm actually crying right now, as I write this, because that day was the day I really met Evan for the first time. I knelt down beside him and looked deep into his eyes. My boy was coming through, I knew it. I felt it with every bone in my body. I immediately ran into the other room and called my mom back in Chicago. It was late there, and I knew I was going to wake her up, but I didn't care. I said, "Mom, I can't believe what I just saw right now. It blew my mind! Mom, he's breaking through. I know it. I know it!"

Dr. Kartzinel had told me there are children who dramatically improve with something as simple as an antifungal, once the overgrowth of yeast is removed from their body. I remember thinking once again, "Yeah, right, if that's the case, why isn't it on the seven o'clock news or *20/20* every night?"

But now I started to believe! It had been only two weeks, and they said it could take as long as six months to be completely done with a yeast problem like Evan's. But with only the little I'd seen thus far, I was willing to go the distance. In the meantime, I decided to find out the connection between yeast, immunity, and autism. Why was Evan's immune system so fucked up? I was inspired and excited about the possibilities for our future. And I was a woman in search of answers.

Chapter 29

࿏

The University of Google

I HONESTLY DON'T KNOW where to begin summarizing all the information I have read and studied. There are many points of view out there, and what you're about to read is mine.

Some children are born with weaker immune systems. Some scientists might say there is a certain gene or enzyme that can be linked to weakened immunity. When Evan was born with a weakened immune system, he couldn't sufficiently process the vaccines the way children who have normal functioning immunity can. So instead of strengthening his immune system, the vaccines were in fact forcing his body to attack itself, which was in turn destroying his immune system. The weakened immune system caused him to be more prone to common illnesses and made it extremely hard for him to recover from them. As a result, he had to take antibiotics repeatedly. The antibiotics stripped his gut, which then caused severe candida buildup, which then caused leaky gut syndrome.

I was amazed by how much information I found. I saw a study done by Dr. Samy Suissa at McGill University showing that the rate of autism increased to a high of 27.3 cases for every 100,000 kids two years after vaccination, whereas of the unvaccinated kids, only 1.45 cases of autism were found. A March 2006 article in the *Journal of American Physicians and Surgeons* showed that when mercury was removed from childhood vaccines, rates of autism dropped by as much as 35 percent.

Sadly, your pediatrician is not going to give you this information. But if many children are suffering in similar ways, how could it not be true? All the other moms I talked to said that their children also had an abundance of yeast, and some children still had staggering amounts of mercury in their little bodies.

Why would vaccine companies believe that vaccines could be safe for *all* children? It's crazy to me. Let's just say a child is born with an allergy to honey, and after a mom gives birth, the doctors rub honey all over this child's body for the next eighteen months. Some bad shit is gonna happen. Then you tell the doctor, "I think my child is allergic to the honey, because his reactions all point to honey." The doctors ignore you, and you think, "Hey, maybe there should be a test to see if some kids are allergic to honey, so other moms don't have to go through this anymore." That is what I would love to have happen from this book. The government can keep giving their vaccines, just give us the test to make sure our babies can handle them. If Evan had been tested for immunity or some sort of enzyme that was vulnerable to vaccines, none of this would have happened. Like I said before, I'm all for having vaccines in today's world; I just believe that the government is obligated to offer a test to help moms know which child can take them—and which child can't.

The stats are staggering. Next time you are in a room with a little over a hundred people, take a good look around. One of the people in that room is going to have an autistic child, and it could be you. My solution can manifest only with help from moms. Strength in numbers, right? Moms are the only ones who can make a difference when it comes to vaccines. If we all said, "I'm going to wait to vaccinate my kid until you test him for immune problems or give me some proof he won't turn into Rain Man," I have a feeling the government would get on it pretty quickly. Many moms I talk to believe too much of what their pediatrician says and still want to vaccinate. I tell them I would at least wait until the kid is eighteen months and make sure he or she is healthy when the shots are given. There is a book I will recommend at the end that might give you a "safer" schedule on vaccinations.

Another theory I have come across is that autism may be caused by an immune system response to a virus, such as a herpes-related virus. A physician by the name of Dr. Michael J. Goldberg has been saying for years that these kids shouldn't even be labeled autistic. He says it's a neuroimmune dysfunction. Take a look at his Web site for more detailed information about this: www.neuroimmunedr.com.

Now, if someone were to ask me, "What, then, do you think is the direct cause of autism? Is it mercury? Is it the viruses in vaccines? Is it a neuroimmune dysfunction? Is it the environment?" I still can't say I know scientifically for sure. But after going through what I did with my baby, I think you can tell I have a weighed opinion. Someone needs to figure out what the hell is going on, or we're going to have much bigger problems then global warming. In the seventies, it used to be one in ten thousand children were autistic. Now it's one in a hundred and fifty. What will it take for people to wake the hell up? One in five children will be autistic, and then what—we can't procreate anymore? If I were a young woman wanting to get pregnant, I would be very afraid . . . very . . . afraid.

Chapter 30

ॐ

Always Ask Why

IF I HAD kept putting a Band-Aid on Evan's health issues, or accepted the downward spiral, as some urged me to do, he never would have begun to heal. It was my dedication to asking questions and researching—WHY his immune system was damaged, WHAT happened as a result, and HOW we can fix it—that led us down the road to recovery. A good example of what I'm talking about is when people get headaches. They go right for the Advil every week instead of asking one simple question: "Why am I getting a headache in the first place? Could it be that I'm hungry?" If they go eat something, the headache goes away. Advil wasn't needed, because they found out the source of the problem. Another great example is that commercial for heartburn. It shows a large man in pain with acid reflux. The company markets a prescription pill to stop the acid reflux, but if the guy just stopped and asked, "WHY am I getting acid reflux?," he would realize that maybe he shouldn't eat an entire pizza and bucket of wings before bed. Voilà, prescription med no longer necessary.

There is also such a huge rise in attention-deficit disorder (ADD) and attention-deficit/hyperactivity disorder (ADHD), with moms being told to medicate their kids. If you looked at what you were feeding your child first, you might not have to medicate them. People tend to think, "How can food change anything?" Well, give your kid a sugar fruit stick or yogurt that has a picture of a cartoon wacky guy on the label, and send him off to school. He's going to be hopped up and acting wild. Sugar and high-fructose corn syrup and artificial flavoring have been known to cause children's behavior problems. My point to you moms is this: Figure out the *cause* for all your kid's issues, and don't settle for the doctor's Band-Aid.

Indigos and Crystals

DO YOU REMEMBER earlier in the book, when I was talking about how I kept pulling out this tarot card that told me to help the Indigo and Crystal children? A woman approached Evan and me on the street and said, "Your son is a crystal child," and then walked away. I remember thinking, "Okay, crazy lady," and then I stopped in my tracks. "Holy shit, she just said 'crystal child,' like on the tarot card." I ran home and Googled "Indigo and Crystal children." It turned out that "Indigo" is a new age term for children who have been labeled with ADD and ADHD, and "crystals" are sometimes autistic children. "Kind of fitting," I thought. I threw myself into learning more and loved the deeper meaning in both these terms.

Chapter 31

Opening the Window a Little Bit More

IN THE MEANTIME, Evan was still excreting yeast out of every part of his body, and every time he did, he would break through more. It was so liberating that I started inviting people back into my house. When my girlfriend came over, she said, "Holy shit, Evan just had a conversation with me." I stood in that moment and relished the confirmation of Evan's healing. It was happening before everyone's eyes. It had been about a month and a half, and Evan was still going through major yeast die-offs. According to my Google degree on yeast, this would continue until his body was a bit more balanced. I knew a big dump of yeast was about to come out of his butt when Evan looked like the Tasmanian Devil. I eventually moved everything I liked to the top shelves so it wouldn't be thrown across the room by a violent yeast-excreting three-year-old.

After another couple of weeks had gone by, Evan's therapist couldn't believe the sudden burst of development. Evan was flying through his programs so well that they couldn't keep up with him. He was social with people and enjoyed having them in his world. Evan was not only starting to feel and think and interact better, but for the first time, he had opened his arms to me and wanted millions of hugs from Mama! Words can't describe the feeling of your baby wanting to be held after years of rejection. These were the visions I'd held on to to during the hard times, and now the visions were coming true.

No more heart monitor, no more weekly fevers, no more itchy ears, and no more tantrums. After John came to visit Evan, he would make comments like "His eye contact and attention were so much better and he's stopped walking on his tippy toes. He's talking so much." John was blown away each month at the progress Evan was making. It was wonderful to watch John and Evan bond during this healing time. Evan was playing so much like a typical kid his age that it was easy for John to relate to him now. I am happy to say that their relationship has bloomed into a beautiful one.

Every day was a miraculous introduction to this wonderful kid who was waking up from a long sleep. I couldn't wait to see what would happen next.

It's Jenny's Turn

IT HAD BEEN a few months since I had walked away from that cute boy with such a heavy heart. During this great upswing, I started thinking about him. Silly high school–like daydreams had gotten me through some icky times when Evan was so sick. Now that Evan was healing and we no longer needed Dr. San Diego and Dr. Texas as much, I decided to text the cute boy in the hope that he wanted to see me. I must have stared at my phone and practiced "Hey, how are ya?" eighty thousand times. I was so scared. What if he'd moved on with another girl? What if he was no longer interested? Something in my heart knew I had to at least try and see what would happen.

"Hey, it's Jenny. Is there still room on your sofa, or has my seat been filled?"

TICK-TOCK-TICK-TOCK-TICK-TOCK.

Finally, I heard a beep-beep and saw that I had gotten a text back: "Your seat will always be here." Hee hee! I felt like a twelve-year-old who'd kissed a boy for the first time and ran over to her girlfriend's, screaming, "He likes me!" I'm such a geek, but I didn't care. After all I had been through, I deserved some happiness. I knew deep within me that he and I were supposed to continue where we had left off. I went back over to his house with a new blouse and a fresh blow-dry and made out with him on the sofa again. It felt so good to be back in his arms; I felt safe and cared for. It was my turn to lean on a shoulder. And what a sexy shoulder it is.

Chapter 32

‿❀

A WOMAN FROM THE STATE HAD COME OVER for a reevaluation on Evan to see how he was improving and whether he needed more hours of therapy. I was so excited for Evan to be evaluated after breaking through. I hadn't told her a thing, I just wanted to see what she thought. I watched her face the entire time she asked Evan to do things. He was not only completing tasks; he was having full conversations with them.

"Evan, can you tell me where this train goes? Does it go in the bowl with the airplanes, or does it go in the bowl with the animals?"

Evan replied, "It goes here," and then threw it in the bowl of transportation vehicles. Then he looked up and said, "I went on an airplane. I went to Canada and saw deer and Santa. Then we went in Mama's trailer, and I played with the fans and ate chips while Mama worked."

The woman from the state department slowly looked up at me and said, "What's going on?"

I smiled and told her to keep testing him. She did all the tests, and Evan not only mastered them but kept initiating conversation and play with her. After the evaluation was done she said to me, "This isn't autism anymore. I don't understand what happened. We have never seen a recovery like this. What happened?"

I replied, "I found the reason for autism, which led me to the solution, and because of that, he was able to absorb the lessons the therapists were giving him."

Now, in no way was Evan perfect in the eyes of parents who had typical children. He would still repeat words a few times and flap his arms, but he was no longer stuck in the world of autism. His bloated belly was gone, and his allergies had become less severe. I honestly believe that if Evan hadn't felt as good as he did, he wouldn't have been able to fully absorb all the intense ABA and speech therapies he was getting. I hope moms pay attention to that. The healthier he became, the more the therapists were able to teach him.

I continue to keep Evan on a wheat-free, dairy-free, yeast-free diet and always will. Some moms bitch that it's too hard to keep up that kind of diet, especially during other kids' birthday parties and holidays. It's a simple solution, really—pack a lunch! I also keep him on ThreeLac, a probiotic that keeps yeast in balance in the gut, and I'll also always keep up with vitamins and minerals. I will continue speech therapy because he could still use some help with conversation—especially abstract language, as he gets older—but for the most part you would never be able to pick him out of a crowd as being a little unique.

I did not wind up doing IVIG blood therapy because I was so happy with Evan's progress that I didn't feel the need. His immune system was stronger—not fixed, but stronger! He did catch flus like other children in his school, but nothing like before. I did do some alternative metal detox that was all homeopathic, and I tried some other scent therapy called mapping. I will leave a list of everything I tried and what I thought at the end of the book.

Also, I decided to take Evan to see an eye doctor for an eye exam on the chance that his weird eye movements and expressions weren't just autism stims. It turned out that Evan needed glasses. He couldn't see because his depth perception was completely off. This happens in MANY autistic kids. They are able to see clearly again with the help of prism glasses and vision therapy. Please look into this for your child. It helped Evan so much.

Something happened yesterday that I want to share. It was Sunday, so it was only me and Evan all day in the house, and I was trying to get some of this book done. Evan would not stop talking to me—to the point where I looked at him and said, "Evan, can you please just stop talking for a whole five minutes today?" And then I stopped and put my hand over my mouth. Wow. Flash back in time, and think about how I had wished and prayed to say that to my kid. Moms say it constantly, and I had always craved it, and here I was, saying it! I got down on my knees and said, "No, Evan, Mama made a mistake. You can talk and talk and talk and talk as much you want, okay?"

He replied, "Okay," then went on to tell me about his airplane unloading passengers at the airport. As I watched him ramble on, tears came to my eyes. I thought about "moo," the most beautiful word in the English language, and about what a journey this has been.

To all those moms of typical children who tell your kid to shut up for five minutes, think twice. You have no idea how much you'd miss the endless talking and questions if they were ever taken away.

Evan is now five years old, and since he is able to completely communicate, I ask him questions that I so badly wanted to know the answers to during the crisis.

"Evan," I asked, "why do you like watching a ceiling fan so much?"

He answered, "Because when it goes round and round, it makes me feel good inside."

"Okay," I said. "I was just wondering."

I watched that little face smile up at the fan and was happy to know that it simply made him feel good. When I asked him why he flapped his arms, he replied, "Because I get SO EXCITED, and then I fly just like the angels do."

How can I argue with that? So he'll take his prom date to the escalators and flap all the way down until sunrise. Sounds like a fun date to me.

NOT ALL CHILDREN with autism will be able to make leaps like Evan. Some parents have worked longer and harder than I have, and with no success, trying the same things. I have no idea why some treatments work on some kids and not on others. But I beg moms *and dads* to at least try. I will work my ass off, raising awareness for autism and banging down doors to get answers. In the meantime, don't give up hope, and remember that acceptance of your child's condition does not mean giving up, it's simply loving your child for being the perfect little spirit he or she is. That was the shift I had experienced before Evan's healing even began. Faith is what kept me moving forward. Oh, speaking of faith . . .

DING-DONG.

Yes, it was the Mormons again.

"Hello, Ms. McCarthy, is now an okay time?"

I smiled at them for a moment and nodded. "Yes, this is an excellent time." I opened the door and let the Mormons in my home. "Go ahead and take a seat, boys."

I sat down next to them . . . but not too close.

As they told me about their religion and how everyone who wasn't a Mormon was going to burn in a pit of flames for all eternity, I saw that their strong belief was extremely warming. They had such conviction and love for their God; I understood why they were able to perform healings that worked for a lot of people. They had faith. I gave them a good forty-five minutes in my home and then thanked them for sharing their beliefs with me. They left me with one of their Bibles, and I watched them walk down the driveway for the last time. Then again, maybe not.

Chapter 33

∽

The Window

I HOPE YOU REALIZE that this is not a book about autism. It's a book about faith. It's the story of a mother who believed anything was possible and never stopped looking for answers. There's still many questions out there that need answering but I want moms out there to have a little bit of comfort knowing I will be searching for these answers so we could someday watch our children lead the lives we dreamed they would have. You can guarantee this isn't the last time you hear from me.

Evan and I will still have our ups and downs, and I'm sure he will always have some obstacle to face, like all of us, but we have faith. And because of faith . . . the window is now open.

TEACH2TALK

Research has proved that video modeling is a very effective method to teach children, and can even teach them skills they may not learn through normal teaching or therapy. Evan learned through watching videos, and I always wished there were DVDs available to teach him critical language and behavioral skills, like playing, answering "wh" questions, sharing, and understanding emotions. Now there are!

Teach2talk's DVDs are developed by a speech language pathologist at UCLA based on published scientific research. I put my stamp of approval on these DVDs, and highly recommend visiting the teach2talk.com Web site to see if any of their videos may be appropriate for your child.

Available at www.teach2talk.com

"What to Do Pamphlet"

∾

WHEN I FOUND OUT Evan was diagnosed with autism, I had no idea what to do. But I knew I had to do something! So I became a detective. Thanks to a ton of Google research, the support of UCLA and my DAN! doctor, and my friendship with other autism moms, I discovered all the organizations, foundations, therapies, and diets that can help pull kids out of autism.

I've created the pamphlet that I wish someone could have handed to me on that fateful diagnostic day. It's intended to point you in a few right directions, to get you started on your own journey of education and experience. I am not a doctor, so I would never recommend any medical treatments or practices, but I have compiled a list of all the doctors and organizations and treatments that have helped Evan and me, and can help all parents navigate autism, under the care of their chosen doctor.

Most important, trust your instincts, and if something doesn't feel right, ask questions.

1. GETTING HELP

When you first think something isn't right with your child, talk to your pediatrician. There are a number of problems kids face that get misdiagnosed, and as you saw from our story, it's crucial to get the right diagnosis as early as possible so you can get the right treatment. In general, most kids get diagnosed with autism before the age of three by a neurologist, child psychologist, or other specialists with credentials. If you are looking for a U.S. neurologist, you can find a list of those who work with autistic children here: www.talkautism .org/TalkAutism/ExpertFind.aspx.

The diagnosticians will perform a number of tests: academic, social/emotional, IQ, and other psychological tests, to name a few. They typically perform a detailed case history and parent questionnaire. They should also order some follow-up medical tests, including: an MRI to scan the brain for abnormalties; a twenty-four-hour EEG to check for seizures and other related issues; and blood tests for rare genetic disorders. Evan saw an audiologist for a complete hearing evaluation because autistic kids often act deaf but have normal hearing. I also took Evan to an eye doctor because autistic kids often have problems wih depth perception. Take a look at www.autisticvision.com. Dr. Melvin Kaplan, O.D., is the best of the best.

2. EDUCATE YOURSELF

I can't overstate how important it is for a parent to read and learn everything about autism. On the Web, you can find great info at TACAnow.org.

Some great books, Web sites, and online communities can be found at:

TACA book list (by category): tacanow.org/booklist.htm
TACA Website list (by category): tacanow.org/weblinks.htm

3. THERAPY AND SCHOOLS

Applied behavior analysis (ABA) therapy has been proved time and time again to really help autistic kids. To get your kid ABA therapy, you need to contact the Center for Autism and Related Disorders (CARD)—centerforautism.com—an organization that provides early intervention across the U.S. Other ABA providers' names vary by state—CARD is the only national organization.

On the site lovaas.com, you'll find a list of national ABA providers. There will be waiting lists, so contact them ASAP.

The California Institute of Behavior Analysis, Inc., at cibainc.org, offers the ABA in-home therapy that Evan received.

Evan's speech therapist can be found at speechsarah@ hotmail.com.

The UCLA Early Childhood Partial Hospitalization Program is where Evan received his first therapies.

Also, I'm about to look into a new therapy I have come across called RDI. Take a look at their Web site: rdiconnect.com.

The "mapping" I talked about earlier that I had done with Evan can be found at unlimitedbrain.com.

It's important to get an attorney who works with autism rights to help navigate the maze of waiting lists and bureaucracy. I know that not everyone has money for an attorney, but he or she can save you money in the end by helping you learn your rights and fight for governmental services and programs. You can find out how to get one of these attorneys here: tacanow.org/legal.htm. An attorney will help you get sometimes twice as much state-funded education for your child. Know your rights!

4. DOCTORS/MEDICAL THERAPIES

Defeat Autism Now! (DAN!) doctors can test for medical issues unique to the autistic child such as yeast overgrowth, food and environmental allergens, mineral depletion and absorption issues, parasite or bacteria imbalance, metal toxicity, and other issues. To find a DAN! doctor, go to www.autismresearchinstitute.com

Look up Dr. Michael Goldberg at www.neuroimmune dr.com to find more about neuroimmune dysfunction.

5. DIET

A lot of people, me included, will tell you that it's important to look into the foods you feed your kids and how they react to them. I know many other doctors and parents will agree that with autistic kids, you should go for an organic and clean diet. It worked for me to feed Evan food that is without additives, preservatives, or dyes.

As you read about in the book, many parents of autistic kids also follow the gluten-free/casein-free (GFCF) diet gfcdiet.com. To learn more about the diet, read *Special Diets for Special Kids Two*, by Lisa Lewis. A ten-week plan to go gluten-free and casein-free can be found at tacanow.org/gfcf_diet_10_weeks.htm.

Supplementation is another common practice to help autistic kids. Again, I am not a doctor, and I would never tell someone how to treat a child's autism, but many DAN! doctors and autistic parents use supplementation because many children on the spectrum often have limited diets, improper food absorption, or severe gastrointestinal issues with chronic diarrhea, constipation or both. I think the best supplementation is from Kirkmanlabs.com. This is where I get Evan's multivitamin, Super-Nu Thera. Another common supplement is mercury-free omega-3 fish oil. Under the guidance of my DAN! doctor, I gave Evan B12 shots. A lot of parents and doctors have noticed an increase in speech after B12 shots. If you want to do B12 shots, you should talk to a

DAN! doctor. To remove Evan's candida, we did start him out on a prescription of Diflucan but after a few weeks, I switched him to a natural supplement that did the same thing. It is called ThreeLac, and if you Google it, you will find many places that carry it. This is the stuff that really made Evan excrete yeast and start talking more. It takes months to get the job done, so be patient and follow the diet rules.

5. VACCINES

I know I have said this over and over again, but vaccines are such a highly controversial subject that I want to state one more time that *I am not a doctor,* and I am not trying to tell you how to treat your child. But as a parent of an autistic child, I feel it's good to be aware of the dialogue surrounding a possible link between vaccines and autism. Some people choose to ignore it, some pay attention. If you're at all worried about vaccines, you should read *What Your Doctor May Not Tell You About Children's Vaccinations,* by Stephanie Cave and Deborah Mitchell. It's really great because it proposes a new vaccination schedule.

6. FAMILY/FRIENDS/A NETWORK OF SUPPORT

Finally, I want to say how important it is to have a network of people who love and support you. Be mindful of the stress on the family, and try your best to make certain everyone is being good to one another. If you have someone in your family or good friends you can lean on, do it! Accept the offers of help. If help isn't offered—ask for it! Reach out to people. When you're in the early crisis period, it can be isolating. But it's best for everyone if you have support. Reach out to other autistic kids and parents. You'll find that they're your best solace. It's so comforting to have people in your life who can relate to what you're going through. And they can be a great source of information on local schools, programs, doctors, therapists. You'll eventually find one another through programs and doctors, but reach out to them. We all need one another!

Some great national organizations offer parent-to-parent assistance. Please check out:

• Unlocking Autism: unlockingautism.org—click on "P2P Network"
• National Autism Associations: nationalautism.org—join NAA and find a friend
• Generation Rescue: generationrescue.org provides "rescue angels" in your area
• If you are in California, go to TACA: www.tacanow.org

For family or friends who are reading this, who don't have an autistic child but have one in their lives whom they love, let me tell you how you can help. The best thing you can ever give is babysitting time. Not pop-in visits—overnight ones! We moms need to get out once in a while and we need help from mainly family, who will say, "Hey, every other Saturday, I will come and babysit all day and all night." That would be a wonderful gift to us. Wow, I can actually hear mothers of autistic children from all over the world applauding right now.

The author will donate a portion of her proceeds from this book to the UCLA Early Childhood Partial Hospitalization Program. The funds will help build additional classrooms so that more autistic children can get the help they deserve.